"It's fitting that God would use Jeff Simmor
and he trusts God more than maybe any o
More is truly his life message. Rolling Hills has seen so many miracles because we ....
leader who has eyes to see. This book will challenge you to trust God and to open your eyes
to see the miracles God is doing all around you. Don't miss the blessing. . . dive in!"

—MARY KATHARINE HUNT
Executive Director of Justice & Mercy International

"*Immeasurably More* will challenge you to make every day better. It's so inspiring!"

–ROBERT D. SMITH
Author of *20,000 Days and Counting*

"*Immeasurably More* clearly displays the Father's love and faithfulness and his track record
since time began. The stories and testimonies are a great reminder that God is ever-present
and active in our lives. Join the journey and open your eyes to God's work in your own life."

—JORGE MHONDERA
Singer /Songwriter /Music Producer

"This book will quickly become a must-read for anyone seeking to grow in their faith and
devotion to living for God. I've known Jeff Simmons for seventeen years and have watched
how his willingness to let go for God and move out in faith led to the establishment and
incredible growth of Rolling Hills Community Church. Jeff is filled with the fruit of the
Spirit and that love, joy, peace, patience, kindness, goodness, faithfulness, gentleness, and
self-control permeates every page of this wonderful book. If you want to know more about
the difference God can make in your life and how he can use you in the lives of others,
please read *Immeasurably More*. You will be blessed."

—MARTY DICKENS
Retired President & CEO- AT&T Tennessee

"This powerful read is for the Christ-follower who feels weary and perhaps is wavering in
his or her faith. My friend and pastor, Jeff Simmons, reminds us that if we can begin again
to see with our spiritual eyes, we will find out that God has so much more than we ever
dreamed or imagined for our lives —immeasurably more!"

—JOHN KATINA
Vocalist, The Katinas

"This book is for anyone wanting more out of their life. I have witnessed firsthand many of the stories and the miracles in this book. *Immeasurably More* will challenge and inspire you to open your eyes to the work God is doing all around you."

—CHARLES OVERBY
Retired chairman and CEO of Newseum and Freedom Forum

"If I were asked to describe Jeff in two words, I would without hesitation say he's a man of encouragement and a man of faith. One of the greatest privileges of my life has been working with Jeff at Rolling Hills Community Church and Justice & Mercy International. This book tells the story of both, but more importantly it encourages each of us to jump into the greater story of God's adventurous call on our lives that is nothing less than immeasurably more. If you need encouragement, spiritual direction, and a greater measure of faith, I recommend this book wholeheartedly."

—KELLY MINTER
Speaker and author of *Wherever The River Runs*

"*Immeasurably More* inspires. Regardless of what you believe, this book challenges you to serve. To hope. To search. Jeff Simmons is a gifted guide for this journey. You will be hard-pressed not to re-examine your life and priorities after reading this book."

—RICK WELDAY
Executive with Fortune 15 company

"If you are doubting the goodness and power of God, *Immeasurably More* is for you. Jeff's amazing stories of God's faithfulness and provision not only gave me chills, they encouraged me to seek what more God has for me in life and reminded me that he is always at work, even when I can't see it."

—ANDREA LUCADO
Freelance Writer

"In his book *Immeasurably More*, Jeff Simmons masterfully brings together truth from Scripture with real-life stories of God at work. What I love most about it is that God is the unquestionable star...and he receives glory on what seems like every page!"

—DENNIS BLYTHE
Executive Pastor, The Church at Brook Hills, Birmingham, Alabama

IMMEASURABLY
MORE

YOUR INVITATION AWAITS

JEFF SIMMONS

Immeasurably More Life Press
1810 Columbia Ave.
Suite 100
Franklin, TN 37064

Ordering Information:
ImmeasurablyMoreLife.com

Scripture quotations, except where otherwise indicated, are taken from the Holy Bible, New International Version®, NIV®. Copyright © 1973, 1978, 1984, 2011 by Biblica, Inc.™ Used under the guidelines of Zondervan. All rights reserved worldwide. www.zondervan.com

In some instances, names, dates, locations, and other details may have been changed to protect the identity and privacy of those discussed in this book.

ISBN-13: 978-0-9974701-0-9 (Hardback)
ISBN-13: 978-0-9974701-1-6 (Paperback)
ISBN-13: 978-0-9974701-2-3 (E-book)

Library of Congress Control Number: 2016946058

Front cover image © Leandro Crespi / Stocksy United

Printed in the United States of America

ACKNOWLEDGMENTS

This is **God's Story**. God has been writing this story, and I am thankful he has allowed us to play a small part. This is all about him. Only God can change a heart and a life. What a blessing it is to be on this journey with him and to share his love and grace with others.

This is also **our story**. This is the story of a church who desires to passionately make a difference for the glory of God in our day and in our generation. This is the story of people who are locking arms together to invest our lives for his great name. We are not perfect, far from it, but we are blessed to be a part of something way bigger than ourselves.

Finally, this is **your story**. Our God is still writing and he is inviting you in on the story. Our God is not finished with any of us yet, and while there is still breath in your lungs, some of your best days can still be ahead. This is the time to turn your heart and soul to Christ and allow him to write a great story in and through you. Your invitation awaits...

Contents

An Invitation

Do you ever feel like you are missing out on how life is really meant to be lived? Several years ago, when my oldest daughter was just four years old, we took a family trip to Disney World. Our two little girls were so excited. It was their first time to Disney! Imagine the joy of a four-year-old and a two-year-old as we flew from Nashville to Orlando.

When we arrived in Orlando, we took a bus over to the hotel. We moved our bags into the room, and then our older daughter, Grace, spied a little playground right outside. While my wife, Lisa, was getting everything ready in the room with our younger daughter, Mabry, Grace and I headed down to the little hotel playground.

Now, this was a very small playground, but Grace loved it. She slid down the slide, spun on the merry-go-round, tried her hand at the monkey bars, and laughed on the swings. We had a great time together!

After about fifteen minutes, Lisa walked out the door with the stroller and announced she was ready to go to Disney World. I picked Grace up and began to cheer, "We are going to Disney World! We are going to Disney World!" This was going to be that moment—the moment where she becomes so excited and throws her arms around me, exclaiming, "You're the greatest daddy ever!"

However, I did not get the response I had anticipated. In fact, Grace began to cry. Then she said, in a loud voice, "I don't want to go to Disney World, Daddy! I want to stay and play on this playground!" I got down on one knee, looked her in the eyes, and quietly responded, "But, Grace, Disney World is like the world's greatest playground! It is so much better than this." All I heard was, "No, Daddy, I want to stay here!"

So many of us live our lives like Grace wanted to that day. God has plans for us that are so much bigger than we can ever believe! Yet, so often, we settle; we want our little playground. God wants us to experience more of life, and we don't want to go.

Lisa and I did manage to get Grace to Disney World that day, and she absolutely loved it! All of us can learn a lesson from her experience. We need to be willing to take the leap from our comfortable playground into the life God has laid out for us. Like in a little playground, we buy into the things of the world, and we settle for a life that is not even close to what God most desires for us. We want to stay with what is comfortable and convenient when God is inviting us on the journey of a lifetime. It is not always easy. The rides are bigger and sometimes scary. It takes courage and faith. But the payoff is incredible!

I pray this book will lead you to experience the fullness of the life God has for you!

So, let's go! Let's start this journey to "more" together. As you read, you will see what God is doing in his church and in the lives of some ordinary followers today. May these stories encourage you and draw you close to the heart of your Heavenly Father as well as to his plan for you. God is your Father. He believes in you and offers you an incredible invitation: to join him in what he wants to do in and through you. God invites you to a life of immeasurably more. Welcome to the journey.

INTRODUCTION

Do you ever look around in life and feel like something is missing? Like there should be more? Do you sometimes wonder what your life is supposed to be like when you "grow up," while at the same time feeling sure that this is not it? There are so many of us that feel this hunger for more. As we search the world for ways to satisfy the hunger, we buy, consume, and chase the latest fads, constantly trying to keep up. Somehow we are never satisfied. Why is that? All of us were created with a longing in life that can only be filled by God. We desperately want to know him and to see him do great things for his glory. We read of miracles in the Bible and we wonder, "Did that only happen back then? Am I somehow missing this today?"

I have counseled people at all different stages of life, all asking the same questions: Is this all there is? Where is God? How can my life be about something more than my to-do list? This book is for those of you who feel that hunger for more in life. Those of you who hunger for more of God. Those of you who desperately desire to experience everything God intended. Those of you who are ready to engage your life in God's greater plans for the world.

People, for example, like Gene and Michele. I met them at church one Sunday morning. Michele told me that both she and her husband were successful in their jobs. They had a wonderful eighteen-year-old daughter, a nice house, cars, and everything that this world seems to offer. But something was missing.

"We know there has to be more."

Right there, I heard it—"more." "There has to be more." By God's grace, I had a front row seat to watch God transform their lives. The family started coming to church each Sunday. Before long, Michele was baptized in Christ, and then Gene and their daughter followed. Their family discovered the more of life as they surrendered to Christ, and they will never be the same. Today, they still have their same jobs, but their joy and fulfillment in life come in the more of God.

Jimmy grew up going to church. He studied the Bible and was always faithful—a great husband, father, and businessman, but there was still something deep down inside that gave him a longing for more. He could not explain it or put his finger on it until he went on a mission trip. On that trip to Moldova, God gave him a vision of the impact he could make in the lives of others for God's glory, and Jimmy came alive! He and his family now sponsor multiple orphan children in Moldova, and his life will never be the same. He prioritized investing his life in what matters, and now his relationship with God has grown deeper, his love for his family has grown sweeter, and his purpose in life has grown richer. As I watch the way he lives today, I know he is living for something more.

Most of us are fascinated by the men and women and the miracles in the Bible, and the differences we see between their stories and our lives today. The people we read about seem to have some quality we don't, and the miracles we read of were often so big and full of glorious mystery. So many of us miss the fact that this same God of the Bible is just as active and involved in our lives today. Maybe you have never thought about this amazing truth. The people and the miracles in the Bible—Moses parting the Red Sea, David defeating Goliath, Jesus healing the sick—called on the same God who is alive and moving today. This same God is constantly at work in our midst—providing, sustaining, and yes, still doing miracles.

The challenge of this life is that most people overlook God and his work around us. We allow our heart, time, and devotion to be consumed by the things of the world that do not satisfy, and we give our praise and adoration to things far too small. Through it all, we miss the God of the universe who is inviting us to open our eyes to what he is doing. If we would allow ourselves to grow deeper in a relationship with God and engage in his work, our lives would be forever changed. Our deep longing for more would be satisfied in Christ. We could trade the ho-hum ordinary life most people fall into for an eternal journey that never ceases to overwhelm and amaze! My favorite verse in the Bible is Ephesians 3:20-21, which says, "Now to him who is able to do immeasurably more than all we ask or imagine, according to his power that is at work within us, to him be glory in the church and in Christ Jesus throughout all generations, for ever and ever! Amen." That is what this book is all about. God desires to do immeasurably more than all we ask or imagine. Yet, so few people ever experience this kind of life. So few ever see God truly do miracles. Can you imagine living a life in which you see God do what only he can do? Can you imagine seeing miracles like back in biblical days? Well, that is the kind of life that God wants for you. Not just more, but immeasurably more.

This book is all about God and what he alone can do! This is the story of people passionately pursuing God and his desire for their lives. This is a story of God's people—not a building or a program, but a movement of this infinitely gracious God fueling his people at a special time and in an amazing way. This is a story about you—about all our God wants to do in and through your life as his follower.

For me, the journey with God began when I was eight years old. There have been many twists and turns along the way, but I can definitely say God is amazing! I have always had a hunger for more—more of God and more of the journey to which he has called me. Every day is exciting when I see God do what only he can do.

I am incredibly grateful for the path on which God has placed me. After working with students for many years, God called my wife and me to plant a church. So in 2003, God brought together a group of fifteen people to step out, plant a church, and begin an incredible adventure with him. What started as a small Bible study grew and became Rolling Hills Community Church in Franklin, Tennessee, just south of Nashville. Little did any of us ever dream what our God was setting into motion for his name and for his glory. This is his story, and he continues to write the script in greater ways than we could ever dream or imagine.

Each of us has a story God is writing on our hearts, and that is why so many of us feel this longing for more in our lives. God is not finished with us. He still is drawing us deeper into his heart and inviting us to be part of his greater story. I pray this book will inspire God's story within you. I pray you will step out, follow God, and watch as he does things you never imagined. I pray you experience God's transforming power in your own life and in the lives of those around you.

Section 1

OPEN YOUR EYES

CHAPTER 1

IS GOD IN YOUR BLINDSPOT?

Our God is doing miracles every day. Most people miss them. We are so busy with our own lives, our own needs, and our own concerns that we miss God moving right in our midst. It is almost as if we are blind to his presence.

Seeing God and seeing miracles requires us to open our spiritual eyes.

Jesus said, "The secret of the kingdom of God has been given to you. But to those outside everything is said in parables so that, they may be ever seeing but never perceiving..." [1] Our ability to see miracles and to be a part of what God is doing in this world requires his supernatural involvement. We need to simply ask God to open our spiritual eyes. Miracles happen when we call out to the Lord God and he opens our eyes to his intervention.

There is an amazing story recorded in the Old Testament book of 2 Kings about a prophet named Elisha. In the Old Testament, a prophet was someone sent to proclaim a message from God. Because God gave him favor and insight, Elisha kept telling the King of Israel the plans for the enemies of the Israelites. Every time the Arameans came to attack Israel, the Israelites were ready because Elisha told them where the attack was going to happen.

Finally, the King of Aram had had enough. He thought he had a spy among his soldiers, but his officers said, "None of us, my Lord the king... but Elisha, the prophet who is in Israel, tells the king of Israel the very words you speak in your bedroom." [2] The King of Aram ordered his men to go capture Elisha. They sent an army with horses and chariots to the small town where Elisha lived with his servant. At night, this army surrounded Elisha's home.

The next morning when Elisha's servant went outside, he saw the entire

Aramean army with horses and chariots! "'Oh no, my Lord! What shall we do?' the servant asked Elisha."[3] You have to admit, this must have been a very scary time for this servant. He thought his life was over. I love Elisha's response: "'Don't be afraid,' the prophet answered. 'Those who are with us are more than those who are with them.'"[4] Can you imagine? The servant was probably looking around thinking, "Hmmm, Elisha must be crazy! An entire army versus just two people? How exactly does this work?" But then Elisha prayed, "'Open his eyes, Lord, so that he may see.' Then the Lord opened his servant's eyes, and he looked and saw the hills full of horses and chariots of fire all around Elisha."[5] Wow! When God opened the servant's eyes, he could see God's army was there ready to fight for them and protect them. The servant went from fear to faith; his heart, mind, and attitude were transformed on the spot.

The story continues. "As the enemy came down toward him, Elisha prayed to the Lord, 'Strike this army with blindness.' So he struck them with blindness, as Elisha had asked."[6] Elisha then led the army right into the middle of the Israelite camp. From there, Elisha prayed for God to open their eyes, and there they were, surrounded by God's army! For us today, the question becomes this: Are we living with fear or faith? Are we living with spiritual eyes to see God working, or are we living in blindness and darkness?

It is so easy to live in fear. At times it seems our whole culture is based on it. Fear sells, so every news program leads with a shooting, a financial crisis, or a tragedy. As fear becomes the lens through which we see life, worry rears its ugly head. We experience anxiety. We can't sleep at night. We fear the unknowns about our health, our jobs, and even our families. Kids growing up in the world today are experiencing intense fearfulness too. Fear cripples us, and it holds us hostage.

In contrast to the ways of this world, God invites us to focus not on fear, but on faith. Yes, it is true there are tragedies in this world. Yes, it is true that bad things happen. But it is also true that good things happen. As God works to redeem all of the hurt and pain in this world for his glory, we can be obsessed with the bad, or we can focus on the good. We determine the lens through which we view life—the lens of fear or the lens of faith.

OUR FALLEN WORLD

We live in a fallen, broken world. When Adam and Eve sinned in the Garden of Eden, death, decay, and pain entered human existence. Before they ate the forbidden fruit, there was no death, pain, hurt, or brokenness, but when sin entered this world, everything changed. Death became a reality. Because of sin, everything in the world moved into a state of decay, which we witness every day. If you plant a garden and do not take care of it, it will get over-run with weeds and eventually die. If you do not take care of your body—water it and feed it well—then it too will decay and die. Hurt and pain entered our world as well, and they affect each and every one of us. People who are hurting go on to hurt other people. The desire to look out for ourselves at the expense of others also began with that bite of the forbidden fruit. Everything gets caught in this spiral of sin.

Yet, here is the incredible truth: Jesus came to bring reconciliation between God and man. Jesus came to mend our relationship with God—to make it beautiful—and to give us life eternal. Furthermore, one day God will make all things right. He will send Jesus to return and say, "Enough! Enough pain and suffering." He will end all evil and take those who are his own home for eternity with him.

So, why does he wait? The Bible tells us, "But do not forget this one thing, dear friends: With the Lord a day is like a thousand years, and a thousand years are like a day. The Lord is not slow in keeping his promise, as some understand slowness. Instead he is patient with you, not wanting anyone to perish, but everyone to come to repentance."[7] God is drawing people to himself so that we all have the opportunity to experience repentance before Jesus returns.

In other words, you and I are living in the in-between—the time between the cross and Jesus's promised return. But God is not taking a nap while we wait. Our God is active! He is redeeming and restoring. He is making things right and making things new. That is God's specialty! He invites us to open our eyes and to see him working all around us.

Just think about it. We can see God in the sunrise and sunset, which demonstrate his faithfulness. We catch glimpses of his goodness in the gift of taste buds and the beauty of colors, both of which magnify his desire for his children to enjoy life. We can also see God in the people around us, who reflect his desire that we never feel alone. God is always watching out for us; we just have to open our eyes to see it.

Jesus told us, "The eye is the lamp of the body. If your eyes are healthy, your whole body will be full of light. But if your eyes are unhealthy, your whole body will be full of darkness. If then the light within you is darkness, how great is that darkness!"[8] Learning to open our eyes to God's work around us brings light to our souls. It brings us into a deeper communion with the God who loves us and who is constantly looking out for us. How awesome it is to think about God opening our eyes and revealing himself in our everyday lives.

WHAT ARE WE MISSING?

How many miracles has God done around us that we have overlooked? How many times has he healed? How many times has he provided financially? How many times has he protected us? How many times has God come through in our lives that we did not even notice? I think the answer to these questions is: far more than we could imagine.

Many times, we miss seeing God at work because our minds are distracted with the things of this world. As humans, what we can see always takes precedence in our minds, but if we are constantly focused on only what we can see with our physical eyes, then we will be consumed with worry, fear, and doubt. By focusing only on our bank accounts, clothes, cars, houses, and the things of this world, we create a false sense of need in our minds and hearts. Everything seems limited, scarce, and temporary. We never seem to have enough. Yet, when God opens our eyes to the spiritual, we begin to understand that our God is limitless. He holds everything in his hands.

In 2 Corinthians, the Bible calls us to live by faith and not by sight.[9] This means we need to stop focusing on simply what we see with our physical eyes and open our eyes of faith. When we do, we will be able to see God at work. We will see him healing, redeeming, restoring, and making things right. We will see God and not just doctors. God uses doctors to bring healing, but he alone is the great physician. God is limitless—he holds the whole world and life itself in his hands. When we open our spiritual eyes, we will not just see a promotion at work with a nice raise, but instead God's provision. We'll see doors open wide, and God beckoning us to be a part of his amazing work in this world. When we open our spiritual eyes, we will not just see friends who reach out in tough times, but we'll see God's love and comfort and support.

SPIRITUAL MARKERS

How many times has God answered our prayers? We pray for people and situations that the Holy Spirit puts on our hearts, but too often we do not open our eyes or take the time to recognize miracles right in our everyday lives. We move on to the next problem, struggle, or worry without ever stopping to recognize God at work or give him a thank you.

The saying goes that hindsight is twenty-twenty. I think this is never as true as it is when we look back for God's work in our lives. We are able to see all the times that God answered our prayers and the different ways God was at work. It is vital that we take note and make those times of God's provision—both in the past and in the present day—spiritual markers of his work and love; we can do that by thanking him.

What are spiritual markers? They are special points in our lives when we claim the truth that we have seen God move, felt his presence, or seen his provision. Establishing these spiritual markers gives us confidence that God will come through in the future. As God opens our eyes and we find more of these spiritual markers, we come to realize that he is greater than anything we could face. What an incredible realization! It allows us to live more faithfully, freely, and alive. As we find more spiritual markers in our lives, we become bolder with our prayers, and we are constantly looking for God to move.

SATAN'S PLANS TO BLIND US

God is always at work in our world today. Our eyes might be blinded to his movements, but he is moving just the same. Our prayers may not be answered in the way we desire or expect, but God is still at work in our lives. His timing is not always our timing and his plans are not always our plans, but our God is present and he is active. He is opening doors, preparing people, and impacting situations in order to bring glory to himself and to transform lives.

When Adam and Eve sinned, we humans, who were created for eternity, began to taste death. Where everything was perfect, a process of decline and decay began. Satan was there to help it along and he continues to destroy people and bring ruin into lives. Here's the thing about Satan: he wants to be equal with God, and this is the spiritual power behind much of the darkness in the world. Because of his vanity and his hunger for power, Satan was kicked out of heaven. He knows he cannot touch or harm God, so what does Satan do? He goes after God's kids. As a dad, I can tell you that if you want to do something to me, that is one thing, but if you go after my kids, that takes things to another level. Satan knows he is ultimately defeated, so he tries to take as many of God's children with him as possible. Misery loves company.

The Bible reveals Satan's plan. In 2 Corinthians it reads, "The God of this age has blinded the minds of unbelievers, so that they cannot see the light of the gospel that displays the glory of Christ, who is the image of God."[11] Satan blinds people. He takes away their ability to see God working. He takes away their desire to see the good that is happening around them. He closes their spiritual eyes.

Jesus says this about Satan: "The thief comes only to steal and kill and destroy..."[12] Satan wants everything to lead to decay. He wants all things to be destroyed. He wants us to feel isolated and alone.

God has other plans. He sent his son to save us from the despair of sin and the attacks of Satan. Even more, God is present and moving among us today. If we want to see God at work in our world, it is not a matter of asking him to act. We need to ask him to open our eyes to all he is doing and ask him to stop Satan from blinding us to his presence. If we become more aware of God's work, each of us will stop seeing coincidences, and instead we will start seeing God. No longer will we try to rationalize things with excuses of simply luck or good fortune. We will realize that "every good and perfect gift is from above."[13]

MIRACLES IN THE MUNDANE

Recently, I was in a very nice hotel lobby. It was massive and open with glass elevators and a ten-piece band playing from the second floor. Music filled the large space. There were chandeliers and sitting areas throughout and a grand piano in the middle. Many people were going back and forth, moving luggage or rushing to appointments, while a few others were sitting in various chairs reading books.

I had a reservation at a restaurant in the hotel and had a few minutes to wait. I was holding my pager and I sat down in a chair in the middle of the lobby to take it all in. As I pondered the busyness of the moment, watching parents wrangling kids, and wondering where everyone was actually going, something amazing happened.

The band started playing, "It Had to be You," and up on the second floor, over-looking the entire lobby, a young man got down on one knee and asked his surprised girlfriend to be his wife. The entire moment was surreal. She was crying tears of joy, the band was playing, and this young man was putting his heart on the line. To make it even better, both of their parents walked into the lobby from different doors and met in the middle. The young man had scripted this perfect scene. The girl, from the second floor, sees her parents, and begins to smile, cry, and wave her left hand to show off her new engagement ring. The young man stood up and mouthed "thank you" to the parents and friends below who came to join in the celebration. It was beautiful.

Yet what struck me was how few people even noticed what was happening. People were going so fast and headed in so many different directions, that they failed to see the beauty or even appreciate the moment. God was bringing together two hearts in the gift of love, there were overjoyed parents who had dreamt of this moment for their children, a band playing beautifully, and everything was orchestrated perfectly—but only a few of those nearby appreciated this life-changing moment. When the band finished, the parents hugged and headed to the elevator to embrace their children.

It was beautiful, sweet, perfect, and God-filled all at the same time—a miracle in the mundane. I often wonder how many of these we miss. How many miracles is God doing on a daily basis that go completely unnoticed? Learning to see God changes the way we live. Embracing his presence in the mundane changes us. We are reminded that God is always at work, and we should not worry or be afraid. God is here. He is constantly moving all around us, and he promises to take care of his children.

Are you seeing God in the good? Are you living with your spiritual eyes open to see his work in your life and all around you?

MOLDOVA: OPENING SPIRITUAL—AND PHYSICAL—EYES

Every year since 2003, Rolling Hills, the church we planted in Franklin, has taken multiple mission teams to Moldova to care for orphans there. Moldova is the smallest and poorest country from the former Soviet Union. The precious orphan children are beautiful, hungry (physically and spiritually), and in desperate need of love and for someone to care. In 2008, we started a nonprofit called Justice and Mercy International (JMI) in order to do greater work in this country that we have grown to love. Since that time at the clubhouse, we have traveled to villages and state-run orphanages. Throughout the years, we have seen God do miracles; he has literally done immeasurably more in the lives of these children and in our lives as well. There are so many stories of life-change for children like Elena, Illie,

Dennis, Tudor, Jazgul, Inga, Alicia, Lena, and more. Every year we meet new children, and we see God work in very specific ways.

In 2012, a couple from our church went on their first international mission trip. When Steve and Lynn signed up to go to Moldova, they were apprehensive. "What is it going to be like? Are we needed? What difference can we make?" Despite all their questions, they felt the invitation of God, so they responded. Along with their two high school children, they boarded the plane to follow God. Little did they know that God would do immeasurably more through their obedience.

The first day at the orphanage, they met many of the kids and had a great time. It was all a new experience for them, but they fit right in. There was one girl in particular who caught Lynn's eye. This young girl looked to be about twelve years old. She sat by herself. She did not interact with the other kids; she simply stared at the ground. Lynn thought she was just being shy. Throughout the day, Lynn saw this girl sitting alone, but she had a hard time reaching out because she was busy with all the other children. Finally, at the end of the day, Lynn spoke to the girl: "My name is Lynn. I will be back tomorrow; look for me and if you want to come hang out with us, you can."

That night, Lynn could not sleep. God kept putting this girl on her heart. The next day, Lynn walked into the orphanage and went straight to her. As the girl sat alone, staring at the ground, Lynn knelt down by her and said, "See, I am back." The girl looked up, and Lynn realized she was blind. One eye was completely clouded, and the other did not focus. Lynn quickly realized why the girl was all alone. She found out her name was Maria, and it was then that God started an incredible work.

The rest of the week, Lynn and Maria were inseparable. Lynn's daughter, Kacey, joined in as well. Lynn and Kacey took Maria to recreation. They made crafts with her. They did everything together. The last day at the orphanage was difficult with a lot of tears shed over the coming separation. Yet Lynn and Kacey had a feeling that they would definitely see Maria again. As difficult as it can be for our teams to leave the orphanage, it is incredibly comforting to know that we have indigenous staff through JMI there to work with the kids throughout the year.

When they returned to the United States, I asked Steve and Lynn to share their experience on a Sunday morning. As they talked about Maria and showed the pictures, there wasn't a dry eye in the place. Lynn said, "We know God has brought us together for a reason."

After the service, a man in our church named Paul Selman approached Lynn and said, "I do not know what it is, but God is asking me to help. I need to do something to help Maria." That started an amazing chain of events in which God did more than we could have ever dreamed. Paul and his wife talked to their eye doctor about Maria. He recommended they contact Dr. Ming Wang in Nashville. Dr. Wang is a renowned ophthalmologist. He is the best in the world at what he does, and he also has his eyes open to God's work in the world. Paul contacted Dr. Wang, who agreed to see Maria if we could get her to the United States.

Finding information on an orphan in Moldova in order to get a travel visa is no small task, yet God handled all of the details. Through the hard work of our JMI National Director, Alina, we were able to obtain a visa for Maria. Flying an orphan from Moldova to the United States by herself was another challenge, but God arranged for some of our people to travel with Maria.

On October 5, 2013, approximately fifteen months after meeting Steve and Lynn at her summer camp, Maria arrived in the United States. It was a huge celebration, and I will never forget that moment. The love shared between Steve, Lynn, and Maria was so evident. The following weeks consisted of consultations and exams by Dr. Wang and his foundation doctors. There were some doubts that anything could be done to improve her vision. It was confirmed that Maria had no sight in her left eye, and there was nothing that could be done to change that. Dr. Wang was willing, however, to try to remove a cataract and replace the lens in Maria's right eye. He made it very clear that it was going to be challenging, but he said, "We have nothing to lose." We gathered around Maria and the doctors and we prayed. We prayed for a miracle and we prayed that whatever the outcome, God would give Maria the grace and the strength to live her life with pure joy.

On November 7, 2013, Maria underwent surgery on her right eye. When Steve and Lynn got her home that evening, her eye was covered with a bandage. Steve and Lynn helped her upstairs to her bathroom and uncovered her eye. Maria looked in the mirror, and a smile grew on her face as big as the country of Moldova! She touched her face, and then she turned and squealed with joy, "Sunt formosa!" ("I am beautiful!") Maria could see herself for the first time in a very, very long time! God had in fact performed a wonderful miracle for this precious orphan from Moldova.

Sight to the blind. It is incredible enough that a blind orphan from Moldova could make it to the United States, but to receive sight is truly immeasurably more than we ever thought possible. God has a way of doing this in all our lives. When we take away the bandages of our past—our inadequacies and doubts—what we find is a God who is full of grace and full of surprises. When we open our spiritual eyes to behold him, we simply smile and we cry because of his glory, grace, and mercy. All glory to a God who loves to do immeasurably more.

After the surgery, God continued to work in Maria's life. Physical sight led to spiritual sight. Maria came to church with Steve, Lynn, and their family, and was recently baptized. She gave her life to this Jesus who opened her eyes to his beauty and his love. This was truly sight to the blind—spiritual, eternal, life-changing sight. And it didn't stop there! Maria now shares her life-changing story with anyone who will listen. She tells them how much Jesus loves them, and that he will walk through life with them if they will only put their trust and faith in him. One seed planted leads to a full crop of souls! This is our hope and prayer for the outcome of Maria's story!

God meets outward needs, but his true desire is always our heart. He knows that unless we change on the inside, we will miss out on what it is to truly live. Our bodies will eventually wear out, but our souls last for eternity.

Our God is always at work—will you open your spiritual eyes to see?

CHAPTER 2

THE INVITATION
OF YOUR LIFETIME

Have you ever received an invitation and felt the excitement of being included? Maybe the invitation was for a special event, and you thought, "Wow! They invited me! I was included. I was chosen." It is an honor and a joy to receive an invitation.

Well, our God has given us an invitation. He is inviting us to be a part of something special; something greater than our own plans and own dreams; something only he can do. We are invited to be a part of God's story. When we think about this incredible gift, we should be filled with awe and excitement! When Jesus began his ministry, he issued an invitation to his first followers. "Come, follow me."[14] Jesus did not say where he was going, how long the journey would be, or how much it would cost. It was just a simple invitation to be with him, an invitation that would change the lives of his followers forever. Those disciples could never have imagined all they would see and do with Jesus. They could have settled for simple, boring lives and died in obscurity, but Jesus offered them so much more—immeasurably more than they could dream! And here's the awesome news: Jesus offers the same invitation to us. If we accept his invitation to follow, we can have a life that gives us a role in what he is doing in this world.

It's one thing to be invited, but it is quite another to commit to go. In Matthew 22, Jesus tells a parable about a wedding banquet. He said, "The kingdom of heaven is like a king who prepared a wedding banquet for his son."[15] (The Bible later tells us that this is exactly what the kingdom of heaven is like because all of eternity will culminate in a giant wedding when the bridegroom, Jesus, comes back for his bride, the church, and a great celebration will follow.[16]) "He sent his servants to those who had been invited to the banquet to tell them to come, but they refused to come."[17] Wait. What? These people were invited, but they chose not to go? If you keep reading, Jesus said that the people who were invited began to make excuses. Have you ever done this, received an invitation and then you made an excuse about why you could not attend? It can be all too easy to do when the invitation causes us some discomfort or inconvenience, or costs us money, time, or even our pride.

In the parable, those who had been invited did not accept the king's invitation, so he sent his servants to invite anyone and everyone! This mirrors the opportunity we have to announce to others the good news that they are invited to God's party! God has given us an incredible invitation. We can make excuses about why we are not able or willing to come and follow Jesus—"I'm busy." "I don't know enough." "God really doesn't want me because of my past." But if we simply make excuses, then we miss out. Accepting God's invitation leads to a deeper understanding of God himself and allows our lives to be richer and more purposeful. We get to play a role in the work God is doing all around us. Being on this journey with him is where we come alive. Miracles happen when we follow God. We see God do what only God can do, and everything in life comes into focus and meaning.

God is inviting you! Will you join in his story?

MY OWN INVITATION

I grew up in a great home. My parents were (and still are) strong, passionate followers of Jesus. They told me early on that God was also inviting me to be a follower of Jesus. I have an amazing legacy of faith that has been passed down through the generations. I will always be thankful for my family, and I am reminded of my personal responsibility to share God's invitation with the next generation.

I was at church a lot as I grew up. I loved being there. My church was one of the first to have a gymnasium, skating rink, and a bowling alley in the church building! I mean, what kid wouldn't want to be there? The facilities really reflected the heart of the church: to reach out to our community and to share God's invitation with others.

The church also had an amazing preschool and children's ministry. As a child, I learned to love and cherish God's Word. This gave me a solid foundation for the years to come. Proverbs says, "Train up a child in the way he should go, and when he is old, he will not depart from it."[18] I am a living testimony to that verse.

All through middle school and high school, I was part of a fantastic student ministry in our church. God put people in my life to teach me the Bible and to challenge me to grow in my faith. Together with great friends whom I still cherish today, I was able to learn, grow, and serve.

In high school, I had an incredible student pastor who was passionate about discipleship and God's word. Along with this, my freshmen year, God moved a doctor from Missouri to San Antonio, and he became our Bible study leader for four years. With a group of about fifteen friends from various high schools around the city, we committed to spending our high school years growing deeper in our faith and to reaching our schools with the love of Christ.

When I was in ninth grade, I first felt God's invitation to something more. I was at a summer camp, and had just left the evening worship, when I felt compelled to pray. I found a little chapel with no one around. I fell on my knees before God and simply poured my heart out to him. I said, "I am yours, God. Whatever that means. I am completely yours." I did not grasp at the time what God was doing, but I knew I wanted to be a part of something bigger than myself.

My junior year of high school, we began hosting a Bible study at my house for kids from my school. Playing on the basketball team and being on student council gave me a platform to invite students from different groups at the school. Over the course of two years, regular attendance at that weekly home Bible study grew to more than one hundred students. By God's grace, we were able to see many students accept the invitation to follow Jesus Christ, and the student ministry at our church exploded during this time.

God was stirring within me a heart for sharing the love of Christ, growing disciples, and raising up leaders. The summer after graduating high school, we took a mission trip to Hawaii. I know, tough assignment. We had planned to go to Israel, but there had been a recent terrorist attack and some of the parents felt that was not the best idea. We had spent a year praying and raising money, so we headed to Hawaii instead.

There are actually some very poor areas on the island of Oahu. We stayed in a small town and worked with a church to share the love of Christ with those in the area. What I discovered on that trip was that inviting people to join in God's story of love, grace, and redemption was the same from Texas to Hawaii. All people matter to God, and all people need God. There was a universality to this Gospel message, and people in Hawaii responded like people in Texas.

Ten years later, in my office in Nashville, a man walked in one day and said, "Do you remember me?" He looked very familiar, but I couldn't quite place him. He introduced himself as James and told me that our mission team had come to his town in Hawaii ten years earlier. He went on to tell me about what happened after our mission trip. The church's youth group, which had been running at about fifteen or twenty students, never dropped below fifty after those two weeks. That group impacted countless lives. In fact, James had just graduated from seminary and was headed back to Hawaii to plant a church. He had two other friends in seminary as well. James said, "God started a movement, and I just wanted to come by and tell you thank you." Wow! I stood there speechless. God truly used our words and time to make a huge impact for his glory. I thanked God, and I hugged James.

I look back at my time in high school as a time of preparation, but also a time of ministry. I truly believe in the saying, "Bloom where you are planted." We cannot simply wait for that big moment to happen. We must engage with the heart of God—loving him and loving others—right where we are. In high school it would have been easy to say we were too young or did not have the right resources or did not know enough. But by God's grace, we saw many people begin a journey with Christ, and God was growing his heart within me through it all.

After graduating from high school, I was excited to go to college. I attended Baylor University in Waco, Texas, and absolutely loved it. (Sic 'em, Bears!) Throughout my college years, God surrounded me with incredible friends, many of whom I still have today. Looking back, I can see now how God was teaching me during that time and preparing me for the future. I was able to learn in my classes while at the same time serving on my campus and in the community. God also gave me some amazing leadership opportunities, where I had a platform to share his love with others, and where he was able to grow my heart.

During my freshmen year, God invited me to be a part of something very special. A man named Louie Giglio started a Bible study for college students in Waco called Choice. For four years, I was able to listen and learn from Louie every Monday night. Louie's passions for worship and discipleship hugely impacted my life.

Since Louie's time at Baylor, God has done incredible things through his life and ministry. Louie built upon Choice to launch Passion Conferences in 1997. These huge annual worship conferences for college students and young adults have impacted hundreds of thousands (if not millions) of people, both in the United States and around the world. In addition, Louie began Six Steps Records as an offshoot of the Passion Conferences, which God has used to shape the worship movement that has occurred over the past several years in churches throughout the United States. It has been incredible to see what God has done through Louie in the lives of so many college students like me. God allowed me to be there at the beginning, and I am so grateful. It's inspiring to watch the faithfulness of one man impact so many for God's glory.

I spent the summer after my junior year studying in London. It was an incredible experience during which the students in my program actually lived inside Westminster Abbey. There was a guard that we walked by every day, and we stayed in dormitory-style rooms attached to the Abbey called Little Dean's Yard. At night, I would walk around the Abbey and pray. I walked by the tombs of kings, Sir Isaac Newton, Oliver Cromwell, George Friedric Handel, Charles Dickens, David Livingstone, Robert Browning, and more. As I walked past the tombs and memorials of these great men, I thought a lot about legacy and the impact of one life on this earth. What would that look like for me? My favorite inscription of all-time is in the Abbey. It is on the tomb of John Laird Mair Lawrence and says, "He feared man so little because he feared God so much." Yes!

During that summer, God gave me a deep hunger for studying amazing scholars and pastors like C.S. Lewis, Charles Spurgeon, John and Charles Wesley, George Whitefield, and others. After reading through their works, I realized that discipleship is more than just studying and reading. There is a responsibility to accomplish what God has put you on the earth to do for his glory. We have to act.

As my time in college began to wind down, I was really unsure about what God wanted me to do with my life. I majored in finance and marketing at Baylor, and my dad was in business and had often told me that I would do well in that field. I wrestled with the feeling that I was supposed to be in ministry, a feeling I had had since ninth grade in that small chapel. I thought that feeling was more of a call to be a Christian businessman— make money, serve my local church, and do ministry and missions in my community and around the world. I always admired these people (and I still do!), and I thought that was the direction God was guiding me. In the midst of the indecision, I felt like I needed to know what I was ultimately going to be doing with my life. It is so easy to forget that our call is simply to be faithful to Christ and allow him to use us for his glory.

When I graduated, all my job interviews were in the business world. I will never forget being in a hotel room in St. Louis and interviewing with Southwestern Bell (now AT&T). After a day filled with meeting different people and learning about the company, I went back to my hotel room exhausted.

As I laid on my bed, I felt the Spirit of God come over me. There's no other way to describe it. I spent the next several hours wrestling with God. I had the distinct impression he was calling me to ministry, and the business world was not the place for me. I reminded him (like he needed to be reminded) that I was only interviewing for business jobs and that I had no idea what it meant to be in full-time ministry. The question of a job and money quickly dissolved into a deeper question of obedience and trust. Would I accept God's invitation to play a different role in his story? The next day, I thanked the men and women at Southwestern Bell for their time and the nice hotel room, but I told them that I felt God calling me to ministry and that I had to trust him. Their reaction was priceless. They were shocked, but also very gracious. I returned to San Antonio not having any idea of what I was supposed to do. I had no job and no clear direction, but I knew that God was inviting me to be a part of what he was doing, and I really did not want to miss it.

So I took a job at a local bank, prayed, and waited. Let me just say that I am terrible at waiting. I want to know the plan. In this case, God was not telling me the plan. When I look back, I can see how God was getting me ready, and at the time he was preparing a place in ministry for me. I learned that, though God's timing is definitely not our timing, it is perfect. Waiting required me to trust in God's faithfulness and drew me even closer to him.

About six months after graduation, the large church that I attended while growing up called and asked me to come work with middle school and college students. My first reaction was, "Middle schoolers? No way. They would drive me crazy." So I turned down the job, but I reluctantly agreed to visit one night to observe. When I walked in the room and saw all the amazing kids, God spoke so clearly and said, "Here you go. This is what I am calling you to do." God's invitation came through loud and clear.

When you find what God created you to do, there is nothing like it! You come alive. I had never before felt the way I felt when I was leading these kids in ministry—completely full of joy and purpose. Over the next few years, I spent a lot of time investing in middle school, high school, and college students. I watched as God drew many kids to himself and transformed lives for his glory. It was a rich time in ministry, and God taught me so much about his love for every single one of us.

In order to grow, God called me to seminary. I knew the general direction of God's plan for my life, so I wanted to be the best I could possibly be for his name and renown. During that time of learning, God gave me a bigger picture of what he was doing in the world and a deeper passion for sharing his love with others.

After graduating from seminary, I had the opportunity to go to Israel to study. The Bible truly came alive for me on that trip. I saw in person all of the places I read about. Walking where Jesus walked made everything even more personal. I could see God's deeper story, from the Old Testament through the New Testament and up to today. My love for his Word and his Son became deeper and stronger.

Following Israel and seminary, I packed up everything I owned in my car and moved to a church in downtown Nashville. For the next six years, I answered God's invitation to be a part of his story by working with middle school, high school, and college students in Nashville. It was an incredible time of ministry, and by God's grace, I was able to invest in some amazing young leaders. Those middle school, high school, and college students have grown into godly leaders who are impacting the world.

Looking back over that time after college through my arrival in Nashville, I can see how God ordered my steps and arranged my experiences to continue to build his story in me—to prepare me for all he had in store. God was slowly inviting me to a deeper faith and love for him.

Through the years, I've had the opportunity to teach conferences and classes. One day, I was guest teaching at New Orleans Seminary, and after the class, one of the professors came up and said, "Jeff, I feel like God has called you to plant a church." His comment caught me completely off-guard. Church planting had never even been in my realm of thinking. However, I knew that when I said yes to God that I was committing to whatever assignment he chose for me.

I came home and started studying everything I could about church planting. One statistic I read was that eighty percent of new churches fail within the first year. That was not very encouraging! God and I had some long conversations over that.

After about a year of studying about church planting, praying, reading, and faith-assessing, I again came to that point of crisis over whether or not I would trust God. I had a great job that I loved, made good money, and I had only been married for a couple of years. When I talked to my boss about this possible call to church planting, his first question was, "How are you going to support a family?" I had no idea. Again, his reaction was not especially encouraging! I had actually never thought about making a live-lihood. I just knew it was coming down to a matter of obedience and trust. I knew God would be faithful, but I was sure scared.

My wife, Lisa, and I knew that God was inviting us to be a part of his story through planting a church. We finally took that step of obedience and trust. I left my ministry position at a church filled with the most wonderful people, and the church said they could give me three months' salary. I was so incredibly thankful.

We moved across town to an apartment complex that had a big club-house where we decided to start with a Bible study on Thursday nights. There were so many questions, worries, and fears as we stepped out in faith to plant the church, but God was present. I realized that there was no place in the world that I would rather be than on this journey with him. I knew God would do something great, but I did not know when or how. I guess that is why the journey is called faith. We must learn to trust God and then watch him do what only he can do! And to get on that journey, we have to first accept his invitation.

Accepting God's invitation to follow Jesus has changed my life forever. God has done immeasurably more than I could ever ask for or imagine in my life. Through it all, I have learned that God is doing miracles all the time. Maybe the greatest miracle takes place inside our hearts and spirits as God moves us from selfish, scared, worried, lost creatures to confident, passionate, and peaceful children of God. Left on our own, we will be far from God and far from his great plans for us, but in complete surrender comes the transformation into what only God can do in us—before he ever does anything through us. What an invitation, and what a God!

Look back at your own story. God never wastes any of the experiences you have been through. He has been actively working in your life since before you were born, inviting you on an even bigger adventure. Can you see how God has been shaping you into the person you are today? What experiences are you in now that could be preparing you for a future God has laid out for you? Open your eyes to his invitation and join in the journey with him.

Section 2

JOIN THE JOURNEY

CHAPTER 3

STEP INTO THE WATER

Recently, our family went on an amazing vacation. We had been saving up for a few years and were so excited. Lisa and I have three wonderful girls who were ten, eight, and five at the time of the trip. As we were planning our vacation, our oldest daughter, Grace, informed us that she really wanted to see a waterfall. I began looking online for opportunities to see waterfalls near where we were staying. I found an adventure tour where you kayak up a river and then do a hike up to a hidden waterfall. The website said it would be six hours round trip, and the reviews were stellar. As Lisa and I discussed this option, we both wondered if Grace would be too young, but we decided to let it be her decision. Every summer, the girls choose one special day just with daddy, and Grace chose the waterfall adventure to be her day.

We had a great start to our vacation, and then the day arrived for our waterfall adventure. We all arose early that morning with a sense of anticipation. Grace and I dressed in our swimsuits, t-shirts, and hiking shoes and applied sunscreen. We stopped for an early morning breakfast at McDonald's, then drove to meet our group.

As we pulled into the gate of a well-worn shack, we parked next to a truck and a trailer loaded with six two-man kayaks. I surveyed the lot and quickly began to realize that we might be in over our heads. There were five other couples, and all of them were in really good shape. As we walked up to the shack, our guide came out to meet us. She looked like she just returned from filming an episode of "Man vs. Wild."

The guide circled us all up and told us that we would be kayaking about an hour and a half up river. The river would be narrow, and we would find a place to pull our kayaks ashore. Then we had about an hour and a half hike through the jungle to finally arrive at the waterfall. She asked, "Do you all know how to kayak well?" Grace and I looked at each other, and then responded affirmatively. As Lisa pulled out of the parking lot in the rental car with our other two kids, I quickly wondered if this was a good idea or not.

A van drove us to the river where we got in our kayaks. Grace was in the front of the kayak, and I was in the back. I knew we would have to paddle fast to keep up with the group. As we were practicing, our guide came by to give us some pointers. I told Grace, "Girl, you better paddle like you mean it." After an hour and a half of hard paddling—with Grace taking lots of breaks to admire the beautiful scenery—we finally made it to where we needed to park the boats.

Grace and I were tired and sweaty as we began the hike. Again, I quickly realized that this too was going to be more challenging than I thought. We were walking through literal jungle, climbing up and over rocks, and stepping through tree roots. Grace and I held hands where we could, and I worked to keep pace with the rest of the group. We were behind, and I could feel Grace's anxiety rising. She fell a couple of times, but she would get up, brush off her legs and tears, and keep going. We were making it until…

We came around a curve in the so-called path only to behold a wide, rushing river. The group was waiting for us, and as we finally arrived, the guide said, "I ran a rope from this side of the river to a tree on the other side. The water is moving fast, so just hold on to the rope and shuffle your way across. The water will come up to your waist, so hold on tightly to the rope." Well, this was the breaking point. Grace looked at me and said, "No way, Daddy! I am not doing it!" With tears running down her face she said, "I'm scared, Daddy!" I said, "Grace, you don't have a choice. You have to do it. We are two hours from anything. You have to go across."

As we faced our biggest challenge yet, I was thinking back to the trip to Disney World when Grace was five years old. I thought she was old enough for the Tower of Terror. Lisa was not so sure, but Grace wanted to go, so off we went. The decision to go on the ride was a huge mistake, but I did not realize it until we are already on it. As the Tower of Terror dropped us in complete horror, Grace was screaming and crying. When we got off the ride, she was still crying. As any good father would do, I said, "I will buy you anything in the park if you stop crying by the time we see Mommy." It cost me twenty dollars for a drawing book that day. However, this time we were out in the jungle, and a quick trip to the gift shop to distract Grace was not an option.

The group started across the rushing river, and Grace and I stood there. She kept shaking her head, "No, Daddy." We were the last ones, and all too quickly it was our turn. "Grace, I love you. I will be with you the whole time, but you have to take the rope and walk." Then, I looked her in the eyes and said, "If you want to see the waterfall, you have to step into the water." With tears in her eyes, she took the rope in one hand. I put my arm around her waist, and we stepped together into the water. One hand over the next, one step at a time, shuffling across, we made it to the other side. "We did it, Daddy!" Grace yelled. The guide and everyone applauded.

The next thirty minutes of hiking were just as challenging, but it was all worth it as we climbed to the top of some rocks and looked across at the most beautiful waterfall I have ever seen. From two-hundred feet above, the water dropped briskly into a beautiful pool. Two spectacular white birds circled above the waterfall. It was like a movie. It was paradise. We walked over some slick rocks until we were able to swim in the pool at the bottom of the falls. The water was cool and refreshing. We splashed, laughed, and played. It was everything Grace dreamed it would be.

On the way back, there was a pep in Grace's step. She talked with the rest of the group and kept up the pace. The lack of a path did not seem as challenging because we had been this way before. When we came to the rushing river, she did not hesitate. She grabbed onto the rope with both hands, and shuffled right across. She helped push our kayak back into the water and paddled the entire way back.

If you ask Grace about her favorite part of our family vacation, she will tell you without missing a beat, "The kayak and hiking trip with my daddy to the waterfall." Every time I hear Grace say that, I remember how scared she was and how she thought she couldn't do it. She knows now it was truly all worth it—the fatigue, the sweat, the fear. She experienced the power to overcome.

If you are going to see the waterfall, you have to step into the water.

Every invitation requires a personal investment. God, in his sovereignty, invites us to be intimately involved in what he is doing. The truth is that God does not need us—he is sovereign—but he allows us to be involved in what he is doing in the world. The great part is that God does all the work. He is not dependent on our finite gifts, but he allows us to be in on the action. God's heartbeat is for lives to be redeemed and for our faith to grow in the process. But in order to see miracles, you have to get your feet wet and your hands dirty. You have to step into the water and into people's lives. It is in this personal investment that your faith grows.

We see this call for personal investment throughout Scripture and in our world today. God's call is his invitation to be a part of his grace and mercy in this world. The Bible tells us, "And we know that in all things God works for the good of those who love him, who have been called according to his purpose."[19] God's work of love and redemption begins with a call to enter into a relationship with him, a call to be a part of his story.

Towards the beginning of the Bible, we meet Abram. He was seventy-five years old when God's call came; "Go from your country, your people and your father's household to the land I will show you."[20] God told Abram that he would do immeasurably more in Abram's life if Abram would just trust God.

Let's think about this. I am sure Abram had questions. "Leave my country and my people to go where? God, can you be more specific? Where am I supposed to go, and what do you want me to do?" You see, we all want God to tell us the whole story. We want to know the details so that we can compare it against our personal desires. But God wants us to trust him—not simply evaluate his plan. God himself is the calling. He is the journey and the destination. Therefore, he says, "Trust me, and go." So many people miss out on seeing God do a great work in their lives because they will not trust God. Abram trusted God, followed his call, and set out for a new home. As a result, he became the father of nations. "In your seed all the nations of the earth shall be blessed, because you have obeyed My voice."[21] That decision to follow God was reflected in God's choice to change Abram's name to Abraham, which means father of many.[22] In the New Testament, God invited a young teenaged girl to be a part of his bigger plan as the mother of the son of God. Mary heard about God's plan from the angel Gabriel and she was scared. She wondered, "How will this be…since I am a virgin?"[23] Mary's first response was to say, "No way. This cannot happen." We so often look at our circumstances and forget about God. We look at our finances, education, or ability, and it all seems impossible. Yet, as God says to Mary, and as he says to us, "For nothing will be impossible with God." [24] Regardless of our circumstances, we must all remember these words: "Nothing is impossible with God."

God wants to do miracles in your life, but you have to trust him. You have to let go of fear and excuses, and realize that nothing is impossible with him. Abraham and Mary both saw God do what only God can do. Your call, and my call, is to simply trust him and watch miracles unfold in your life.

I believe God still calls people today, just like God spoke to me in that hotel room in St. Louis while I interviewed with Southwestern Bell. God speaks to people all over the world. God is drawing people to his heart, and he is inviting us to be a part of something way bigger than we can imagine. How many people hear his call but never respond? Whether the fear or excuses win out, something keeps them from truly living sold out lives for Christ. Think about how much they have missed. Think about how many miracles they would have seen if they would have only trusted God and embarked on the journey of a lifetime.

I will never forget when I told my boss that I was feeling God's call to plant a church, and his first question was, "How are you going to support a family?" I stood there speechless. Through all the planning, prayer, and preparation, I had honestly never thought about that. But once he said it, I could not shake it. Was I crazy to take this leap? I experienced doubts and struggles; questions and fears plagued me, but whether or not we planted the church ultimately came down to a matter of obedience. If God indeed was calling me to do this, then I had to trust that he would provide. I did not have to have all the answers, but I did have to respond to his invitation. I needed to take a step in faith and make a personal investment in all that God was calling me to do.

Lisa and I decided we could live off her salary for the first year or two while the church was getting started; the idea of my wife supporting us was a pride issue I had to overcome. We set a budget, asked people to help, and prayed like crazy.

That time was one of the most faith-filled of our lives. Yes, parts were hard, but Lisa and I were following God's call, growing in relationship with him, and trusting him to provide. It takes faith to grow in your spiritual life, and faith means recognizing that you do not know all the answers. Faith means trusting the one who calls rather than trying to constantly control your outcomes. God is more interested in growing our dependence on him than he is in our personal, worldly definition of success. When we walk in faith, we see God do miracles, and in the process, God is the one who receives the glory.

God is also more interested in our obedience than our comfort. Sometimes we can be in the center of God's will and still go through challenges. This is how our faith grows. Outside of salvation (that is by grace), it is in the challenges that we become who God is shaping us to be. We struggle in order to grow and become stronger. God wants to grow our faith. It is not always easy, but it is always worth it! Why does God do things this way? Why do we have to make a personal investment and trust him? Why doesn't he just tell us the plans or the outcome? For one thing, we probably would not believe God even if he told us his plans because they would be more than we could imagine. More importantly, he receives the glory in doing things this way. When we trust God and take a leap of faith, we realize we could have never accomplished our goal on our own, so it had to be God. Everyone else recognizes this as well! God's name is lifted up and praised! All glory is given to the one who deserves it.

What about you? Where are you in your relationship with God? Is there something God has been calling you to do that you have continually been afraid to explore or for which you continue to make excuses? Maybe it is leading a small group Bible study. Maybe it is going on a mission trip. Maybe it is adoption. Maybe it is a new career.

I don't know what it is for you, but I do know this—when God invites you to join him in the journey, you can be assured that the best is yet to come!

A RETIREMENT THAT DOESN'T QUIT

Steve Norris was just a normal guy. His priorities in life were simply work and his family. He came to church when it was convenient, but never became truly engaged. Not too long ago, Steve's company was sold, and he was able to retire early. Being the dad of three boys in middle school and high school, he thought this was the perfect opportunity to spend more time with them. Yet, when his kids were at school, he began to wonder if there was something more he should be doing.

Every Sunday when Steve was at church, he experienced a nagging feeling. For four to six weeks, he dismissed it and went on enjoying his new retirement. Then in one Sunday message, he heard this, "If you have a nagging feeling, it might be the Holy Spirit trying to get your attention," and it clicked. God had something else for Steve to do, so he began praying, talking to other people, and asking God what he might want him to do.

A few weeks later, we began a "Next Steps" initiative at Rolling Hills. During this initiative, we asked everyone to take a next step in their spiritual journey, whatever that step may be—baptism, international missions, sponsoring an orphan through JMI, serving in local missions, or something else. We called the people in our church to be obedient. For Steve, that next step was to help young men. From previous work experience and living life as the dad of three boys, Steve knew about the importance of men stepping up to be leaders. He felt God guiding him to help young men take that step.

Steve contacted the YMCA and found out about a residential program called Y-Build. In this program, the Y helped young men who were just getting out of prison or had tough upbringings to get jobs. Steve asked if he could get involved as a mentor. After a few weeks, Steve's eyes were opened to the needs and the hardships these young men faced. God showed Steve that the Y-Build program was a place where he could really make a difference.

Steve was heartbroken when the YMCA decided to close the program due to finances only a few months after he had gotten involved. However, Steve knew those young men needed a chance and an opportunity if they were ever going to succeed in life. Then, God spoke to Steve and said, "You take this over." Steve thought, "No way. What do I know about running a non-profit?" Again, God spoke to Steve. "You take this over." And, again, Steve offered excuses as to why he was not the right guy. Finally, God spoke to Steve again. At that point, it was not about knowing what to do, but simply a matter of obedience. God was calling Steve to make a personal investment, to take a leap of faith.

With some help, Steve took the program over. He changed the name to 4:13 Strong, based on Philippians 4:13 which says, "I can do all things through Christ who strengthens me." The YMCA generously donated the use of some of the facilities to Steve, a normal Christian guy who was now in charge of a residential program for young men. He had to raise money, set training schedules, secure jobs, and pray like crazy. His entire life shifted overnight, and yet looking back, it seemed like it was what God had planned all along.

After a few months in his new role, Steve was excited, but still feeling a little overwhelmed. However, 4:13 Strong was working! God had provided financially, and many young men were keeping jobs and making huge strides as husbands and fathers. Lives were being changed, but there were still some guys who would drop out, show up late for work, and make poor choices. Steve was realizing the challenges of ministry as well.

One day on, as Steve describes it, "one of those down days," his cell phone rang. He did not recognize the number, so he didn't answer. Then he wondered if someone was in jail or if something was wrong, so he checked his voicemail. When he listened, he heard a message from a young man in the program. The message was, "Mr. Steve, this is Anthony. I just want you to know that I love you. If you have ever wondered if you are making a difference, then just look at me. I love my job, and my life will never be the same. Thank you." Isn't that just like God! Anthony had grown up in New Orleans. He saw his mom get shot when he was only seven. He ended up in juvenile detention at the age of ten. Anthony got out, but ended up back in prison when he was seventeen. In his twenties, he was released from prison and became a gang leader in Memphis. Life had been hard.

One night in Memphis, Anthony walked into the gang house and just stopped. He thought, "Is this where I want my life to be?" There was a small church down the street, so he went there. The pastor told him, "You need to sell everything, buy a bus ticket to Nashville, and go be a part of 4:13 Strong. I guarantee it will change your life." Anthony left, went to an abandoned house, and thought about what this pastor had said. The words, "I guarantee it will change your life" played on repeat in his head. The next day, Anthony sold everything, bought a bus ticket to Nashville, and became a part of 4:13 Strong. His life was forever changed because of his step in faith.

Steve tells of Anthony calling him one day. Anthony was bursting with excitement because he had been able to buy a friend lunch at the gas station. When he was leaving, Anthony realized that the cashier had given him too much change. He said, "The old Anthony would have walked out thinking he won the lottery, but I remembered something I learned in the 4:13 Strong program: 'Character is who you are and the decisions you make when no one is watching.' So I went back in and told the cashier that I had received too much money, and wanted to give it back." After hearing this, the cashier went to get her manager.

The manager asked Anthony for his ID. He thought he was in trouble. The manager went in the back and made a copy of it. He then came back out and gave the photocopy of Anthony's ID to the cashier and said, "Look at this picture. Any day this man comes into this store over the next two weeks, give him anything he wants under twenty dollars." Then he said to Anthony, "Young man, one of my best cashiers lost her job last week because her drawer did not balance. This young lady would have lost her job too without your honesty. Thank you." Anthony was blown away. He couldn't wait to tell Steve that doing things the right way really worked! Because of Steve's faith, Anthony's life has been forever changed. Anthony was baptized, loves his job, and is making a difference in other men's lives. Steve also impacted the lives of so many others in the program, and the lives of innocent people who could have been impacted through bad decisions made by some of these men had they not joined 4:13 Strong. Steve's family and friends have been impacted as well by witnessing Steve's decision to step out in trust and live life for God. Steve was obedient to God, and is investing his life for God's glory. He did not settle for the easy life, but instead he answered God's call. When you invest personally in what God is doing, He does immeasurably more.[25]

Do you have a nagging feeling? Is God trying to get your attention? Listen to him and invest your life for his glory! Your obedience (or disobedience) leaves an impact on your life, and the ripples will affect your family, friends, and people you do not even know yet. Everything God has been doing in your past has been preparing you for your future. The best of your life is still to come. Trust God, and invest your life for him today! You can't even begin to dream about all God can do through you, but it will be better than you can imagine. I guarantee it!

CHAPTER 4

GOD BEGINS WITH WHAT YOU HAVE

One of my favorite stories in the Bible is the feeding of the five thousand. Jesus was preaching to a large crowd, and as the day drew to a close, his disciples wanted to send people away so they could get something to eat. Instead, Jesus asked the disciples what food they could find to share. All the disciples managed to gather was one small basket of food, offered up by a young boy, containing five loaves of bread and two fish. Jesus took that food and asked the disciples to share it with the crowd. They walked throughout the hillside, sharing food with everyone there, and at the end, they gathered up twelve baskets of leftovers. It was a miracle![26] It is easy to concentrate on the miracle that happened that day, but what I love is the little boy who simply offered Jesus his lunch. That little boy did not have a clue that God would use him as part of a miracle. He was simply sharing—seeing a need and meeting it with the resources he had. His simple act of giving and trusting sparked a movement that impacted thousands, a movement that we still speak about today. God does not need us, but he invites us to be a part of his story, and he does not ask for more from us than what we have.

Twelve years ago, Rolling Hills started with that Bible study on Thursday nights in the apartment clubhouse. The first night, there were fifteen people—only fifteen—gathered together and praying; we had no idea what God was going to do. God had given us big dreams about sharing Christ with our community and ministering to the poor and forgotten in our world. The odds seemed overwhelming, but we took our little and simply put it in Jesus's hands. Today hundreds of families have partnered with our church, which now meets at two campuses. Who would have ever dreamed how God could do immeasurably more than all we asked for or imagined? I think back to the people who were there that first night in the clubhouse. Two of the single adults ended up getting married to each other. Today they have two kids and an amazing family, and God is using them to build his church at Rolling Hills. Another single adult is now a missionary in India. A couple that was there that night is in full-time ministry with university students. Another couple has a business that has done really well, and they are using the resources to fund ministries locally and around the world. For every person who was in the clubhouse in those early days, God has done "immeasurably more." It does not mean there have not been challenges, or that everything has been perfect in everyone's life, but every person would tell you that God has been so faithful, gracious, and surprising along the way.

Thinking back, we did not have any experts in church planting, nor did we have a lot of money. We were just ordinary people who were willing to listen and follow God. We were passionate about serving Christ, and we believed that God could take what we offered and multiply it. Our hearts were burdened to share Christ with our community and to grow deeper in our personal faith journey, and God exceeded our expectations.

TRANSFORMATION

One of the first few days in our new apartment, I went to work out in the apartment fitness facility, where I met a guy wearing an Indiana shirt. I asked him, "Did you go to Indiana?" He responded, "When Bobby Knight threw the chair, he missed me by ten feet." (Bobby Knight was the men's basketball coach at the University of Indiana who famously became so mad at one game that he threw a chair across the court.) We laughed, and that started a great conversation. Tyson later told me that he had been a cruise director in St. John's and had recently moved to Tennessee. His ex-wife lived in Franklin, so the move made it much easier to be with his two kids. I invited Tyson to our Thursday Bible study.

The next week, Tyson came walking into the clubhouse. He listened and seemed to enjoy the meeting. The following week, Tyson came back. This time he had a Bible. He said, "I didn't have a Bible, so I just went and bought one." He showed us his new Bible with his name engraved on the cover. He took so much pride in having his own copy of God's Word.

What unfolded next was amazing. I watched as one of the guys in our group—a man named Dave who had grown up Catholic, leaned over and said, "Can I see your Bible?" Tyson handed him his Bible, and Dave said, "Tyson, look, you have a concordance in the back."

"What's a concordance?" Tyson asked.

"If you want to know more about prayer, then you just look up 'prayer' and all the verses about prayer are listed. It's the same way with any word—'worry,' 'trust,' and more."

Tyson said, "Wow! I got the deluxe version!"

Our God was inviting Tyson into his bigger story, and Tyson went on to give his life to Christ. I still remember Tyson's baptism. Even more amazing is that not only was Tyson baptized, but ultimately both his kids were baptized as well. To this day, Tyson is serving faithfully on Sunday mornings at church, directing traffic in the parking lot with his son. God took a little and is impacting generations.

Also in the apartment complex, Lisa and I met a young woman named Emily. She had recently graduated from speech therapy school and was working at a local hospital. She lived upstairs with her roommate, Allison. Emily and Allison started coming to church and became involved in our small group. Emily was one of the first to hold our brand new baby, Grace, when we came home from the hospital.

As the church grew, we moved out of the apartment complex, but we still saw Emily and Allison each week. One Sunday a few years later, Emily invited her boyfriend, Jason, to join us for church. Jason wore a suit (the only guy in the place with a tie on), and he stood over on the side for the entire sermon. I thought, "Man, this guy is skeptical." While Jason was a bit skeptical—he had never been to church inside a movie theater or to one with drums and electric guitars—I found out later that he stood because he had back surgery and could not sit down, but Jason kept coming.

As weeks went by, Jason, Emily, and I began having spiritual conversations. Jason had a lot of questions, yet I could clearly see God working in his life. I will never forget the joy we all felt when Emily and Jason were baptized. Before long, I had the privilege to officiate their wedding. A few years later, we were at the hospital celebrating the birth of their son. Today, they are faithfully serving the Lord and they are amazing leaders. Again, we can look at their lives and see God impacting generations.

When calling us to join in his story, God always starts with obedience, not outcome. As humans we tend to want God to tell us the outcome before we decide if we want to be obedient. In essence, we want to take what God offers and then compare it to our own desires. We want to consider it as one of many options, but God wants us to trust him. God will always do immeasurably more than we can ask or imagine, but we have to trust him, offer what we have, and step out in obedience. Do not sit on the sidelines or make excuses. God wants to do something great through you, but you must accept his invitation and place your life in his hands.

ANNELIESE AND BEST BUDDIES

Anneliese grew up in Canada and was actually on the Quebec Rugby team. (This is amazing because she is very petite, gentle, and still has both of her ears!) After college, Anneliese moved to Las Vegas and was working at one of the major hotels as a nutritionist. One day, a guy named Chandler was in Vegas for a business meeting and saw Anneliese; it was love at first sight—for Chandler, at least. He went to the dietician's office on one of his break times and asked to make an appointment because he "really needed help with his diet." The plan worked, and in three months Chandler and Anneliese were married and moving to Nashville for his job.

One Sunday morning, just a few weeks after they had moved to Tennessee, Chandler and Anneliese were driving to get breakfast, when they saw signs for Rolling Hills. They decided to come in and check it out. Chandler had attended church as a child, but Anneliese had not. They connected with people at Rolling Hills on that very first Sunday and started consistently attending. A year later, they welcomed their first child, a beautiful, healthy baby girl. Two years later, Anneliese became pregnant again.

This pregnancy was different. The doctors informed Chandler and Anneliese that their son had Downs Syndrome. The news was devastating to them at first. They did not understand how this happened and felt so much fear, doubt, worry, and concern. They both knew they wanted to keep the baby, but what would life be like now? Chandler and Anneliese went through the different stages of grief from denial to anger to sadness and every feeling in between.

On the day Matthew was born, he was immediately rushed into heart surgery. In addition to intellectual and developmental disabilities, children with Downs Syndrome often have defects of the heart and lungs, and unfortunately Matthew was no exception. Anneliese recalls thinking, "I wonder if it would be better if he did not live." Those thoughts are difficult for her to imagine today, but they were real at the time. Matthew was fighting for his life, and his parents, along with an entire young church, were praying for him.

Anneliese fell in love with her little boy, and after multiple surgeries, Matthew was doing better. He was finally able to come home from the hospital, and life with a child with Down Syndrome became the new normal for Chandler and Anneliese. Anneliese remembers that her first concern for Matthew was not his developmental delays, but rather whether or not he would ever have any friends.

During this entire time, Chandler and Anneliese were in our small group. One night while we were meeting in Bible study, Anneliese announced that she heard about a program called Best Buddies. It was started by Anthony Shriver, whose mom started the Special Olympics, and it was for children with Downs Syndrome and other developmental delays. Anneliese talked with such passion about how the group pairs up a highly functioning student or adult with a developmentally delayed student or adult, so that they have a "buddy." Anneliese said, "I want that for Matthew!"

The problem was that there wasn't a Best Buddies program in Middle Tennessee. Anneliese called the organization and learned that it would cost $250,000 to start a program. I will never forget the night that Anneliese said, "Where in the world am I going to get $250,000? I am a stay-at-home mom. I have a child with Downs Syndrome. We're just trying to make ends meet." She began to cry. It was a God moment. We all prayed together, and I could just feel that God was about to do something special.

Anneliese put it all in God's hands—her life, her time, her money—and she went to work. There is nothing like a mom on a mission! She was fighting for her child, and God started opening doors. One of those doors flew open through the Nashville Predators hockey team. The coach at the time, Barry Trotz, also had a child with Downs Syndrome. Anneliese connected with him and others, and within a few months she had raised more than $200,000! Anneliese's passion became not only for Matthew, but for every child with developmental delays in Middle Tennessee. She started the first Best Buddies chapters at one middle school and one high school. Then she started a chapter on one college campus, and she set a goal to reach every school in the state.

Only five years after the state office opened in 2010, Best Buddies in Tennessee is on twenty-four middle school campuses, seventy-five high school campuses, and fourteen colleges in the state! More than fifteen-hundred students and adults with intellectual disabilities attended the Best Buddies Prom last year at the Bridgestone Arena in downtown Nashville. Anneliese was named the director of Best Buddies of Tennessee and continues in that role today. The growth is unbelievable, and so many lives are being impacted for good.

Beyond the number of people who have been involved in Best Buddies programs, it is incredible to see how Anneliese is changing the culture. In the past, children with intellectual disabilities were picked on and made fun of in school. Kids can be tough sometimes, and the words used were hurtful. But now, there is a movement where kids are sticking up for their friends with intellectual disabilities, desiring to be their "buddy," and even electing them as homecoming kings and queens. The faith and passion of one mom is changing the culture.

Anneliese has changed from someone who was so scared to someone who has allowed Christ to change the world through her. This is what God loves to do! We are just called to take the little we have to offer and place it in his hands.

What is amazing is how our obedience to Christ impacts more than just us. Anneliese just wanted Matthew to have a friend, yet God was doing so much more. He knew there were others who needed help, and he was just waiting for someone to step up and make a difference.

What do you have to offer? Your response to God's invitation impacts more than just you. Think about that. Whatever God is asking you to do will have a huge impact on you, but may be even more important for people you have never met. A simple act of obedience can change someone's life for eternity. When you see a need, meet it. Do not make excuses. Do not come up with all the reasons something will not work. Put your faith and your life into the hands of Jesus and watch him multiply it for his glory. Spiritual growth is not about knowing all the answers, but about faith and trust in the one who is the answer.

CHOOSING PURE JOY - SARA EZELL

Sara was born on November 11, 1971, at seven pounds. Soon after her birth, she was diagnosed with Osteogenesis Imperfecta, a very rare bone disorder sometimes called brittle bone disease. Though the diagnosis looked grim, Sara and her family were determined to overcome. Sara gave her life to Christ at a young age. Although she spent much of her life in a wheelchair, and never grew past three feet tall, Sara chose to live a God-centered life and not let her disease hold her back. She offered up her heart, her gifts, and her life to her God.

Sara graduated high school and was accepted into Vanderbilt University, where she graduated Magna Cum Laude and received her Master's degree in Special Education with a 4.0 average. Sara began working with children with disabilities and served as Disabilities Services Coordinator for Vanderbilt University students. In that role, Sara impacted countless lives for the glory of her great God.

Every Sunday, Sara taught preschoolers at Rolling Hills. Kids loved her! Many kids would ask why she was in a wheelchair, and she would brilliantly respond, "God gave you legs, and he gave me wheels." Sara taught those young children that all people matter to God, and God can use all of us to accomplish his will.

Not only did Sara use her gifts to help people at church and work, but she also faced all parts of her life with joy. Sara made the most of her years, and God used her in an incredible way. She inspired us all by teaching us that joy is a choice. Happiness is an emotion, but joy comes from the Lord. Each time I saw her, no matter the circumstances, Sara was full of joy and making the most of her one life. At least three families named a child after her. Multiple couples were put together by her matchmaking. She taught thousands of children between her job at Vanderbilt Children's Hospital and her role in the preschool ministry at our church. Sara lived joy. I never heard her complain. Even though we all knew she was suffering, she never made life about her; instead, she always laughed, smiled, and gave joy to others. When Sara was in the hospital, the chancellor for Vanderbilt University came by to see her because she had made such an impact on the university community.

During a celebration at Rolling Hills, we asked a few people to paint a word on canvas that described their relationship with God and present their work to the church. People painted "Savior," "Redeemer," and "Healer." And then Sara rolled on the stage in her wheelchair. She had painted "Joy" with a smiley face. There was not a dry eye in the place.

Sara died in 2014 at the age of forty-three, but she would want you to know that she is alive and well. She has traded in her old, brittle body for a glorious new body. I am sure that she is in the middle of a huge group of children, laughing and dancing in heaven. She is doing backflips down the streets and singing at the top of her new lungs. She has no more pain and suffering. She is healed, and she is alive!

Sara always taught me that whatever you offer to God, he can and will use for his glory. Sara gave her life to Christ, and God used her to impact the world. There are so many people who are unencumbered by wheelchairs or diseases, but do so little for God and for others. They focus on what they do not have instead of what they do. I praise my God for the life of Sara Ezell! So many lives are deeper and richer because of her. May we be inspired by her legacy to never give up and to know that nothing is impossible!

God wants to use what you have to do his work in this world. He wants to use your heart to reach the lost and the broken. He wants to see the things that break your heart and give purpose to your passions, so you can help bring this world the hope and healing it so desperately needs.

We sense when God is calling us to move, but so often people say to God, "I can't." We hear the call, but cannot get past what we do not have. "I don't have time." "I don't have any talent." "I don't have money." "I don't have great charisma." In the process, however, we forget about what we do have—a really big God who is for us, a God who loves us, a God who can and will do immeasurably more.

When we live with an "I can't" mindset, it keeps us from living the amazing life that God has laid out for us. There comes a point where we have to bring our "I can't" thoughts to God and place our life—all of it—into his hands. When we do, God gets excited because he loves to respond, "You are right—you can't, but I can." That is where the fun begins! I could go on and on with stories about the lives of people at Rolling Hills—men and women who have trusted God and seen him do incredible things. People like Mary

Katharine, who felt God's call to leave a high-paying job and take half her salary in order to head up a non-profit. Today, she is the Executive Director of Justice and Mercy International, and through JMI, she is impacting orphans, the poor, and the forgotten. She is seeing life change on a daily basis because she put her life in the hands of Jesus and trusted him to do what only he could do.

Or someone like Saundria Keck. She did not consider retirement from a successful career as the end of God using her. Today, Saundria is still actively involved in our church and heading up a ministry impacting hundreds of women. Through Mom2Mom, she is helping moms with young children at a time in their lives where they most need encouragement, reassurance, and prayer. Saundria is impacting generations and having the time of her life! Or Mark and Alva Duke. When we started Rolling Hills, their daughters were in high school and college. They had an empty nest on their mind, but God had other plans. Today, Mark and Alva are the parents of two other "daughters" who were former orphans from Moldova. They continue to be leaders in church, and now have six grandchildren actively involved in the Rolling Hills' preschool and children's ministry. Mark and Alva trusted God with their lives, and he is truly impacting generations through them.

There is incredible power when you take what little you have and put it in the hands of Jesus. Don't offer excuses or think what you have is too little, but truly trust that God can and will do immeasurably more. The best of your life is still ahead, so have faith that God can take what you have— your gifts, talents, abilities, resources, experiences, and more—and use it for his glory. Put your life in the hands of Jesus and watch him do miracles!

CHAPTER 5

WHERE IS YOUR FAITH?

Everyone believes in something. Every culture that has ever existed has had some form of worship. Why? Because our souls know there is something or someone bigger out there. Even people who say they do not believe in God believe in something, whether it's themselves or some scientific theory. Now, I do not believe that God and science are mutually exclusive. God created the world and he created a dynamic, changing place of growth and beauty.

God did not just set the world to spin and then back away. He is actively involved in our lives. Think about that. The same God who created the world "ex nihilo" (a Latin phrase meaning, "out of nothing") is the same God who is actively involved in your life today. There is nothing he cannot handle.

So where is your faith? What do you believe about God—about who he is and the role he plays in your life? I believe it takes more faith to not believe in God than to believe in God. Seriously, think about it. Where did all this come from—the earth, space, all of the lives around us, and where is all of this leading? Real-life miracles happen every day. We can see miracles unfold before us as God provides food for the hungry, redeems the hurt of divorce, brings together communities to support and love each other through this life, and more. God is constantly at work, and he is inviting us to join in! He is inviting us to be a part of something bigger than ourselves. How can we do that? How can we accept God's invitation and jump in to be a part in his story?

JUST ASK.

That's it. There's no trick or secret. We just have to ask God to lead us to take up our role. God even tells us, "Ask and it will be given to you..."[27] God wants us to ask.

When we have hard times, instead of relying on our God and spending time in prayer to ask for his help and guidance, too often we try to fix things ourselves. We work so hard on our own, trying to be independent and sometimes making an even bigger mess. When we get to the realization that we cannot fix our problems ourselves, then it seems that we are willing to call out to God for help. But what if we didn't function this way? God is always there for us. We could save ourselves so much heartache and struggle if we would just ask for his help and guidance, if we would just reach out to our father who loves us first. Instead, we strive and flail and worry. Worry costs us so much sleep and unbelievable amounts of stress. Can we instead lay our worries at the feet of our Lord and take comfort in trusting him?

Think about how you pray. What do you say? It is easy to ask for help with day-to-day problems because we see them right in front of us. "God, can you please help me get through this day?" "God, can you please help my body to heal, so I can kick this cold?" "God, can you please help my child sleep through the night?" Nothing is wrong with these prayers, but what are they saying about what we believe about God, who he is, and how he moves in the world? Do we only trust God with the smaller details of our lives? These simple prayers can easily become the full extent of our prayer life. While it is important to pray about everything, it can become easy to stay on the surface, to be afraid to go deep. We are scared to pray for God to move because the question looms, "What if he does?"

And he will. God will move and he will ask you to do big things. But he will also provide! He'll provide the energy, the time, the creativity, and the resources. He has shown himself to be faithful. How many times has God bailed us out of tough situations? How many times has he provided financially? How many times has he come to the rescue? We need to remember his love and faithfulness, and we must call to mind the spiritual markers of our lives. How many times have we just moved on to the next crisis, situation, or struggle, never stopping for a moment of thanksgiving or to see those answered prayers as an opportunity to grow in our faith?

When God invites you to ask, he wants you to trust him with all parts of your life. We need to trust God for who he is and trust him to move, not just in the small parts of our lives, but in the big parts as well. We need to pray—beyond our every day—for things like the salvation of a family member or friend who is far from God, the healing of a marriage that seems beyond hope, or for spiritual revival to come to our community. When we fight for our lives, our families, or our communities through prayer, we are able to step into the work that God is doing in this world.

So I ask again, where is your faith? Do you see the role God is playing in your life each and every day? Do we love God even if he does not answer our prayers just the way we want? Do we love him for who he is? God loves us more than we even love ourselves. This needs to be reflected in our prayer life as well. Sometimes our prayers are more self-centered and not what is ultimately best for us. The best answer for us is not necessarily to win the lottery or to drive a Porsche. We may think that more money will solve all of our problems, but many times it simply amplifies the problems we have. We do not need more money; we need more of God! Being a dad, I see this type of asking on a daily basis. My girls will ask for chocolate almost every day after dinner. My youngest daughter, Kate, loves "midnight chocolate" (dark chocolate). She would eat a dark chocolate Milky Way for every meal if we would let her. However, would I really be a good parent if I said, "Sure! Go on! Indulge!" every time she asked? No way. We all get this, but sometimes we forget that God is our loving Heavenly Father. He knows what is best for us.

Of course, we think we know what is in our own best interests, but we really don't. We cannot see what will happen next week, next year, or ten years down the road. What looks like the right answer for us now may have huge consequences later. It really does come down to having a heart of faith and trusting that God knows what is best for us. A mark of spiritual maturity happens as we learn to pray like Jesus, "God, not my will, but yours be done."[28] Through prayer, God invites us into the journey. He allows us a front-row seat for the miracles that he will do. As the great missionary William Carey said, "Expect great things from God. Attempt great things for God." Many times this attempting comes in the asking and expecting.

THE ANGEL AT THE MOVIE THEATER

After three months in the apartment clubhouse, Rolling Hills had outgrown the space. We prayed and asked God to open a door to a new place for us. The Marriott Hotel was just down the street and seemed like the perfect location for our growing church to meet. At first, the hotel management was not open to the idea of a church renting the ballroom on Sundays, but we kept asking and praying. When they called to tell us that we could use the space, we were so excited! We thanked God, and we prepared to move to the hotel.

Our time at the Marriott was great. God brought more people, and we continued to see lives transformed for his glory. One of my favorite parts of being there was doing baptism in the indoor swimming pool. We would walk down after worship and all gather around the pool. Sometimes there were people swimming, and we would invite them to watch as we welcomed new brothers and sisters in Christ. It was such a special time.

One day about six months into our time at the Marriott, the coordinator at the hotel called me up to deliver some disappointing news, "Next week we have an Amway Convention, so you guys cannot be here on Sunday."

Hmmm. We have five days to find a place to meet, I thought. *What are we going to do?* Pray.

We prayed for God to help us, and he did. That Sunday, we met in a barn, seriously. It worked for the week and the horses were pretty calm during worship. However, our challenges were not over. Getting kicked out of the hotel ballroom for other events became a regular occurrence. Our church met in a bridal shop and any other place we could find. The joke became, "If you can find us, you can worship with us."

After about a year, the events coordinator at the hotel called me to say,

"We have conventions February 7th, 14th, 21st, 28th and March 14th." When she told me this, it was already the middle of January! We started to panic and pray. We knew our time at the Marriott was coming to an end, but where could we go on such short notice? How could we continue to reach people if we did not have a regular place to call home? The options in our area were limited. Each time we had been moved out of the hotel for special events, we reached out to a few places in town that would fit a larger number of people and be available on Sunday mornings. We were always turned away. Now that the final countdown was on for our time in the Marriott, we tried again.

There is a movie theater in the center of our community that seemed to us like it might meet our needs. In the past, the general manager had said our renting the theater would not work. He said the regional manager did not allow churches to meet in their theaters.

We only had a couple of weeks left at the hotel, and we were out of ideas. But here's the thing about God—he is never late. His timing is not always our timing, but God's timing is always perfect. In fact, it is in the waiting (and praying) that we learn to trust him. So we continued to pray and ask God to provide a place for the church to meet.

The week before our last Sunday in the hotel ballroom, I was praying, and God said, "Go to the movie theater's regional headquarters and talk to them." So I did. I drove to the regional office, walked in, and asked for the regional manager. The administrative assistant, Tera, said, "Well, our regional manager has just been reassigned, and we have a new regional manager." "Really? Can I see him?" I asked. She replied, "Actually, today is his first day, so he is really busy. He just moved here from Texas." As she said this, the new regional manager looked out of his office door and hung up his phone. I walked right toward him and said, "You're from Texas, and I'm from Texas. Welcome to Tennessee."

For the next twenty minutes we talked about Texas, kids, and life in general. Finally, I said, "Thomas, let me tell you why I am here. I am the pastor at a young church, and we need a place to meet. We would love to meet at your theater in Franklin." He said, "Well, before I moved we had just started renting out theaters in Texas. I will have to call our corporate headquarters in Atlanta to find out if it will work here. When do you need to know?" I replied, "Well, today is Wednesday; we need to know by Friday or Saturday because Sunday is our last day at the Marriott hotel." "Are you serious?" Thomas asked, but he agreed to look into it. We shook hands, and I left.

On Saturday, Thomas called. "Okay, you got it. As long as you are out of the lobby by 10:30 in the morning, you can have half the movie theaters until noon." Woohoo! I was pumped! I thanked him profusely. Then I called our worship leader, and we celebrated on the phone together. During our services the next day, we said, "Everyone say good-bye to the Marriott; we are moving to the movie theater!"

Here's another great part of this story: Thomas was only in Nashville for three months before he was promoted to a new position in Atlanta. I believe God brought Thomas to Nashville just for us. Only God would be so creative as to send an angel disguised as a regional manager of a movie theater.

MOSES WAS WILLING

The Bible is full of people asking God for help. Let's think about Moses. He was an answer to the prayers of the Israelites living in Egypt. You see, at the time, the Israelites were living as slaves to the Egyptians. They were ruthlessly forced to work in horrible conditions. Beyond that, the Pharaoh did not like that their population continued to grow, so he began to order the death of all baby boys born to Israelite women. Can you even imagine what life was like? The people cried out to God to save them from the oppression they faced.

God heard their prayers and sent Moses to lead his people out of slavery. Moses, however, did not jump at the chance to lead. When God spoke to Moses through a burning bush, calling Moses to lead the Israelites from Egypt, Moses' immediate reaction was to feel unworthy and offer excuses. "But, God, what if they do not listen to me?" "But God, I am not a great speaker." Instead of being excited and embracing the call God had on his life, Moses made excuses. Those excuses were a cry for help.

When Moses asked God for help, God answered in two ways. First, God promised to always be with Moses, just as he has promised for all of us! Then he also sent Aaron, Moses' brother, to join him as the speaker to the Israelites.

Moses returned to Egypt, and God used him in a powerful way. Through Moses, God brought ten plagues upon the Egyptians to deliver close to one million slaves out of Egypt. God led Moses and the Israelites on a journey through the desert to the Promised Land. Moses invested his life, and God did immeasurably more than he could have imagined!

THE START OF JUSTICE AND MERCY INTERNATIONAL

As you have read, when God called us to plant Rolling Hills Community Church, we started with a handful of people meeting in an apartment club-house. Even at that Bible study early on, we knew we wanted this young church to be a part of something only God could do. We wanted the church to reach far outside the walls of our building, and we wanted missions to be at the core of who we are and what we do. Early on, we established that we wanted to take a mission trip, but we weren't sure where we felt called to go. We asked God to give us direction, and he sure delivered! At the same time our Bible study was starting, a friend of mine, Steve Davis, was working for an organization in Texas. As we were talking one day, he told me about the country of Moldova. My first question was, "Where's Moldova?" Steve shared a lot with me about the history of this Eastern European country between Romania and Ukraine as well as its poverty. Then he dropped the statistic that God used to break my heart. Steve said, "About sixty percent of the girls trafficked into prostitution in Eastern Europe come out of this country of four million." It was as if God was shouting to me.

Steve told me about the work his organization was doing in the orphan-ages in Moldova. He described the grim conditions of the orphanages be-cause of the poverty of the entire country and talked about how these were some of the most vulnerable children in the world. I knew we had to do something. Nine months later, we took eighteen people on our first mission trip to Moldova. Little did we know what God was starting in our hearts as well as in this country.

The first trip was life-changing, just as my sixteen subsequent trips have been. The eighteen of us were moved to tears by the impoverished conditions of the state-run orphanages and the overwhelming needs among the boys and girls we met. The children were dirty, wearing the same shirts and shorts each day, most of the time with no shoes, and the only toilet was a hole in the ground. The kids were crammed into small barracks, many sleeping two to a bed—with the bed being a single cot. Each child had one box for personal items, and many of these small boxes were not full.

At the same time, we fell in love! Our hearts came alive in the joy of the precious orphan children who literally clung to us. We experienced God in a way we never had before, and we saw Christ among the poor, the broken, and the lonely. We each had a new depth of knowing God's heart and his love, and we will never be the same.

After taking teams to Moldova multiple times a year for the next few years, we knew we had to do more. In 2008, Rolling Hills started our own non-profit called Justice and Mercy International, or JMI. We realized that, as a church, we would be limited in our reach, but as a non-profit and an NGO (nongovernmental organization), we could establish crucial partnerships and do even greater work. We believed that God could use JMI to do incredible things, and the impact has been amazing! By God's leadership through JMI, we have been able to establish two transitional living homes in the capital of Moldova—one for girls and one for boys. Most children have to leave the orphanages at the age of sixteen, though many graduate at fifteen and move out. They have no place to go. The statistics are staggering about the number of orphan girls trafficked and the number of boys who either end up in organized crime or commit suicide after they leave orphanages. Adolescence is the most vulnerable time in those children's lives, and we had to do something. The transitional living homes provide ways for us to help protect these children. Each home has a two-year program to disciple kids in Christ, teach them employable skills, and help them become responsible leaders for their country. The results are incredible! In addition to the transitional living homes in Moldova, JMI is now working in more than ten state-run orphanages with hundreds of children being sponsored by people in the United States. It is amazing to see the difference a sponsor makes in the life of a child. Sponsors provide clothes, food, and needed healthcare items through our JMI in-country staff. We now have twelve full-time and part-time native staff in Moldova to work with the children, including a national director, psychologist, social worker, house parents, and a vocational placement official. In addition, sponsors in the U.S. send wisdom, encouragement, and life-direction to vulnerable children through email. It is awesome to see what God is doing through JMI in the lives of so many.

JAZGUL—SHE ASKED, GOD ANSWERED

JMI's impact is most evident in the stories of individual children who have been touched by their work.

Take Jazgul for example. Jazgul was born in Kazakhstan. Her father left Jazgul, her mom, and her sisters when she was very young. Her mom could not afford to keep the children, so Jazgul and her sisters went to live in an orphanage. However, one night her mom decided to sell her daughters. She picked them up at the orphanage. Jazgul remembers being a small child waiting at a train station. But by the grace of God, her mom could not pull together the money to purchase the train tickets to get the girls to the city where she could sell them. In her frustration, Jazgul's mother took her daughters into the countryside and found an old, abandoned school where she tried to starve them. Jazgul remembers crying out to a God that, as she says, "I did not even know yet."

Through a series of miracles, some people in a nearby village found the girls. They were able to get them to an orphanage. The director of the orphanage accepted the girls and began taking care of them. Jazgul would lay in bed and wonder about all that had happened to her, but somehow, she says, "Inside I knew that God had a plan for my life."

As Jazgul got closer to her fifteenth birthday and the time to leave the orphanage drew near, she would lay in bed and pray. She had nowhere to go, nothing to do, and no one who seemed to care. Yet, in her heart, she would cry out to God.

As only God would have it, Jazgul graduated from the orphanage and met our JMI National Director in Moldova. She invited Jazgul to live in the Grace House, the transitional living home for girls in Chisinau. A young woman from Rolling Hills named Ingrid was on one of our mission trips to Moldova that same year. She met Jazgul and offered to sponsor her stay in the Grace House. Now this young, vulnerable child began to see that she had a "hope and a future."[29] During her time at Grace House, Jazgul met this God to whom she had spent all these years praying. She trusted Jesus Christ as her personal Lord and Savior and was baptized. From there, she went on to learn English and enrolled in additional schooling. Jazgul then began to serve other children in local orphanages as well as at the Grace House. She became a quiet leader, growing in her faith and using her abilities for God's glory.

In her heart of hearts, Jazgul kept calling out to God. She wanted to study in the United States, which seemed like an impossible dream, but she asked God anyway. Jazgul never stopped dreaming and asking as she remained faithful where she was at the time. Her faith in God kept growing, as did her willingness to serve him. She was able to look back on her life and see that she truly was a miracle. God had done amazing things in her life.

After she graduated college (America's equivalent to high school) in Moldova, with the help of Ingrid and a lot of other generous people, Jazgul was accepted to a university in Nashville. Her dream of studying in the United States was coming true! She boarded the plane and, with tears into her eyes, stepped into the life that God had planned for her.

Today, Jazgul is excelling as a student at Lipscomb University. She is learning so much, growing daily in her relationship with God, and going back to Moldova during her summer vacations to serve in the orphanages. She intends to move back to Moldova when she graduates in order to impact the lives of other orphaned and vulnerable children. She asked God for the impossible, and he did it, but she is quickly realizing that this is just the beginning of God's plans for her!

In an apartment clubhouse, we would have never dreamed what God was going to do. We simply asked God to allow us to be involved in his global story. It is incredible what will happen when you ask God to do something big. Pray big prayers and trust God to accomplish his will.

There are endless stories of people asking and God providing. God hears prayers and wants to move according to his will and for his glory. He acts in the lives of people like Moses, people like Jazgul, and people like you and me.

Examine your life. Are you praying prayers that are small for a great God? Are there prayers that you are scared to pray? Trust in God to guide and provide. Ask him to do great things for his glory in you and through you, and your life will never be the same. **Just ask.**

CHAPTER 6

HIS MIRACLES OUTRUN OUR DREAMS

Ask and it will be given to you; seek and you will find; knock and the door will be opened to you. For everyone who asks receives; the one who seeks finds; and to the one who knocks, the door will be opened. Which of you, if his son asks for bread, will give him a stone? Or if he asks for a fish, will give him a snake? If you, then, though you are evil, know how to give good gifts to your children, how much more will your Father in heaven give good gifts to those who ask him![30]

In chapter seven of the Gospel of Matthew, we hear Jesus speak the words above. Through these verses, we get a glimpse of God our Father. He provides for us, but he wants to do more—so much more!

When God performs miracles, they are always *so much more* than we could ever dream. Like when we read about twelve baskets full of food being left over after Jesus fed thousands with a few fish and three loaves of bread, or when the disciples caught so many fish that their nets broke. When God acts, he goes over and above. God loves to surprise his people and bless them beyond measure. Luke 6:38 says, "Give, and it will be given to you. A good measure, pressed down, shaken together and running over, will be poured into your lap."

Each time God provides in such amazing ways, he also asks us to trust him. We need to trust him not only to provide for us, but also to be the God he tells us he is. We need to trust that God can move mountains, can redeem hard situations, can perform miracles, and so much more.

THE BLESSINGS OF THE PROMISED LAND

One of the clearest examples of God blessing people beyond their wildest dreams is the gift of the Promised Land. God first mentions the Promised Land early in the Bible when he makes a covenant with Abraham in Genesis. God promises that Abraham's descendants would take possession of their own land; they would come out of slavery and be blessed with a homeland. God maintained this covenant with Abraham's son Isaac, his son Jacob, and all of their descendants.

Four hundred years after Abraham, God's people were enslaved in Egypt. When the Israelites were finally able to leave Egypt, not only did they leave slavery behind, but they also left with riches from the Egyptian people! God stayed with the Israelites, leading them through the desert to the Promised Land. The Lord had already blessed them above and beyond what the Israelites could possibly have imagined, but there was still more to come.

When the people finally arrived at the land God had promised, they sent twelve spies into the land to learn more about it and the people living there. It was not just land; it was so much more. The spies brought back pomegranates, figs, and a cluster of grapes so big that two men had to carry it on a pole between them! The spies took these fruits back to the people of Israel where they testified, "We went into the land to which you sent us, and it does flow with milk and honey! Here is its fruit."[31] In spite of all the miracles the people had seen when they escaped from slavery and the incredible blessings of the land, the people still did not trust God enough when it came to driving out the people currently living in the land, and they lost their faith. But God wanted his people to experience his blessings, so the Promised Land was not lost. The people wandered in the desert for forty years, and when the time came, God again led them to the Promised Land.

On the cusp of entering the land, Moses spoke to the Israelites, reminding them of their God who loved them and wanted to bless them with so much more than they could dream, prompting them to be faithful to a God who never fails. "When the Lord your God brings you into the land he swore to your fathers, to Abraham, Isaac and Jacob, to give you—a land with large, flourishing cities you did not build, houses filled with all kinds of good things you did not provide, wells you did not dig, and vineyards and olive groves you did not plant—then when you eat and are satisfied, be careful that you do not forget the Lord, who brought you out of Egypt, out of the land of slavery."[32] This time, a new generation of Israelites trusted God. Joshua led the Israelites into the land, and they were able to drive out the people who lived there. The people trusted, and God provided so much more than they could have dreamed.

FROM WAREHOUSE TO WILDEST DREAMS

I have witnessed God move and provide so much more than we could ever imagine for his people and his purposes.

I've already described how, as a young church, Rolling Hills was blessed to find worship space in a local movie theater when we could no longer meet at the Marriott. We met in that same theater for five years. Each week, a team of volunteers arrived at the church at 6:00 in the morning with a trailer full of supplies. We brought everything with us each week: our sound system, signs, baby beds, rockers, carpet (Have you ever seen a movie theater floor?), supplies for kids, and even extra diapers. We had to be out of the theater by noon, which meant that as soon as we said, "Amen," everyone had to grab something—a baby crib, a rocking chair, a sign, a speaker—and take it to the U-Haul. It was truly all hands on deck. It was hard work, but we rejoiced in God's provision for the space.

It is incredibly hard to believe that through all of that time, we never had a rental contract with the movie theater. It was always a week-to-week rental, spanning through the terms of multiple general and regional managers as well as countless theater employees. Any one of these managers could have kicked us out at any time.

Of course, this is not an ideal situation for a church over the long-term. Each week we would pray like crazy because we never knew if we would have a place to meet and worship, but God knew. We trusted him, and he sustained and provided.

After our third year in the theater, it became clear that it was time for the church to start looking for another place to worship each week. We were maxing out the facilities at the theater with our worship auditorium and childcare areas. In addition to that, the strain of the weekly set-up and tear-down was beginning to take its toll on our dedicated volunteers. Along with this, we sometimes got to view movie trailers that inadvertently started during the sermon. This was a little distracting as I was teaching about love or grace, and a trailer for *Transformers* or *Resident Evil* drowned me out.

As we began to look around for a new space to meet, our possibilities were scarce. We were out-growing yet another rented facility, but building our own space seemed incredibly out of reach. Land in the Franklin area was selling for nearly $800,000 an acre! We were a church less than five years old, and the average age of people regularly attending on Sundays was just twenty-seven. The tithes and offerings we brought in each week covered facility costs, outreach, staff, and missions, but we did not have any extra money to buy land and then build the infrastructure; it seemed out of the question. For us to make a move would definitely require a miracle! We prayed about our future, talked with people, explored our options, and trusted that God would provide. One day, a member of our finance team called me and said, "Jeff, I have a client who owns a warehouse that he is putting on the market. Do you think we would be interested in looking at it as a possible place to buy for a church building?" A warehouse, or really anything already built, was not something we had considered, but the idea was intriguing, and we were definitely willing to talk.

I went with Larry Atema, a member of our leadership team, to the warehouse to meet with the owner. The warehouse was 143,000 square feet, sitting on just over twelve acres, and south of downtown Franklin. We could have never imagined something so huge. I mean, it was enormous! It was the old Georgia Boot Factory, but it had sat empty for years. When I say "empty," think wide-open, clear-span industrial space under a twenty-four-foot roof with huge, roll-up dock doors. It was definitely God-sized! Although all of that open, empty space was a bit overwhelming, we began to get a vision of how it could work as a church building.

We left the meeting knowing that the building would be a great fit for our church. There was only one problem: how could we ever pay for it? The list price of the building was several million dollars.

When we met again with the owner, we discovered he was a Christ-follower. He said, "When I bought this building, I had a feeling that God was going to use it someday for his purpose. I just never knew what it would be." He then told us that he would give us some money off the purchase price because he believed in what we were doing. This was great news! However, the building would still cost several million dollars, and we simply did not have any money. We shook hands with the owner, parted ways, and kept praying for a miracle.

A few months went by, and the idea of somehow using the warehouse as a new home for the church would simply not go away. God was at work, but we could not figure out what to do. We prayed, we brainstormed, and we talked to experts. Finally, our staff and leadership decided to go to the church members and ask for a one-time offering. We called it "Wildest Dreams." We asked everyone what their wildest dreams would be for a church facility, and then we asked everyone to pray big prayers to our God.

Everyone at Rolling Hills approached the offering with a sense of anticipation. We told people, "Just bring what God leads you to give, and let's see what he will do." We prayed, we stretched, we trusted, and we all personally invested. There is something amazing about joining your life with like-minded, godly people who want to invest all they can for the glory of our great God!

The offering Sunday came, and I remember feeling excited. I knew that no matter what happened with the offering, God would show us the way to help the church continue to grow in order to impact more lives for Christ.

I will never forget that Sunday. The church was not filled with multimillionaires, but ordinary young adults, parents, and kids. The dream of moving to the warehouse seemed impossible from our perspective, but we never forgot about God! People sacrificed—pulling from savings, retirement, and friends—and we put it all into the hands of our really big God. In that one Sunday, the church gave one million dollars! On paper, there was no possible way that could happen. It was the miracle of the fish and the loaves all over again. God took what little we had and multiplied it for his glory. The story of his faithfulness and blessing that day still sends chills up my spine. To be a part of something like that was absolutely incredible! The offering was enough for us to make a down payment on the building, so we scheduled a meeting with the owner of the building to ask if he was still willing to sell. When we arrived, the owner was happy to see us, but he said, "I did not think you all were interested, so I went out and found three tenants. I was going to simply lease out the building. I have not built out the tenant spaces, but I have signed leases."

"Well, would you still sell us the building?" we asked.

"Yes."

Then we asked, "Will you include these leases if we agree to build them out?" He again agreed.

"And will you still give us the same discount that you offered earlier?"

He thought for a moment, and then said, "Yes."

We had our miracle! Rolling Hills bought the huge building we now call home, and God supplied the money for a down payment plus three tenants whose lease payments would cover seventy percent of facility costs. We called the place The WareHouse, and it is an amazing place of worship and ministry. Who could ever script that? Only God! As God loves to do, he did immeasurably more! The WareHouse was so big that we could build out the tenant space and still have close to 90,000 square feet of space for the church. This was more than enough for us—so much more. In addition, one of our new tenants was the State of Tennessee Department of Children Services, which meant all foster care for our county would come through our building. This was awesome for ministry to children and families in need. Plus, having the other two tenants meant that there were people we could minister to throughout the week.

I believe this God-orchestrated arrangement could be a new paradigm in ministry. As the price of land and buildings goes up all around us, what if this is the model God begins to use in order to grow other churches? What if this is a new way we can engage with our world—churches and multi-use sites refurbishing existing facilities and bringing hope to the community around them? Imagine the difference we could make as we see the partnering of churches, business, government, and education to serve the poor (physically and spiritually) in our neighborhoods and throughout the world. This is truly so much more than we could have ever imagined!

THREE-ON-THREE

When we first started Rolling Hills, we talked about how to best connect with our community. There was a man in our church named Ken Thomas. As he and I discussed ideas of how to reach out, we realized that our town was passionate about sports, so we thought about doing a three-on-three basketball tournament in the middle of our community. We dreamed of how great it would be to see children, students, and adults having a great time and connecting in the love of community and Christ.

There was one small problem: we didn't have any money. Our church was less than a year old, and we were using every dollar for rent, children's equipment, and material for Sundays.

We went and met with the local owner/operator of Chick-fil-A, Bill Pfaender. He was kind and gracious to meet with us. As we shared the vision for a basketball tournament with him, Bill said, "I have been thinking that we need to do something great in our community." He then offered to sponsor the event with $5,000! Wow—this was amazing! The local movie theater agreed to let us use their parking lot for the tournament, and we came across a guy from Indiana who rented basketball goals. This God-given vision was starting to come to life.

Two days before the tournament, we had only one team signed up. We had advertised all we could, but it was not working. We had a great group of volunteers lined up, but everyone was discouraged. Ken and I met to talk about canceling the event. As we talked and prayed, we really sensed God saying, "Go forward and trust me."

The next day, we put everything in place for people to come, and come they did! The day of the tournament, we had forty-one teams, and the "Cool Springs 3-on-3 Basketball Tournament" sponsored by Chick-fil-A was born! It was amazing!

The next year, the event grew. We added more teams and a Family Fun Zone. The following year, there were even more teams, a bigger Family Fun Zone, and a concert. We used the entire parking lot at the movie theater and shared the love of Christ with so many. The church was growing, and we were connecting with families in our community in the joy of Christ.

By the third year, another man in our church, Gabe Norris, had become an integral part of the event. Together, Ken and Gabe began Connect Ministries with a desire to build upon the success of the three-on-three tournaments and connect churches with their communities. God has done amazing things through the two of them.

One day, Ken and Gabe drove to the corporate headquarters of Chick-fil-A to present the idea of doing basketball tournaments in partnerships with local Chick-fil-A restaurants in other cities across the United States. The meeting went well, and the Chick-fil-A executives loved it. The executives then went on to pitch their own idea to Ken and Gabe: camps for kids.

Today, Connect Ministries runs camps for kids in conjunction with Chick-fil-A. They also run basketball tournaments and races in communities all across the United States. This year, Connect Ministries had over 23,000 kids at day camps and many more at basketball tournaments, races, and other events. We had no idea that Rolling Hills would someday give birth to ministries like Connect. God gave us a vision to connect with our community over a common interest and we simply said yes. Ken and Gabe had a vision to expand the ministry and make an even bigger impact across communities, but they could have never dreamed that God would grow their vision into what it is today. They have an office with over twenty full-time staff and three hundred college students serving alongside them in the summer. They are impacting lives and transforming generations for the glory of God.

I often think back to the night we were thinking about canceling that first event. Hearing God say, "Go forward and trust me." changed everything for us, and it can change everything for you. Maybe God is saying this same thing to you today—"Go forward and trust me." God wants to do great things in your life. Don't get distracted and don't give up. Go forward in Christ and trust that he will accomplish his purpose in you. The best is yet to be.

GOD'S SPEED—FROM TWELVE TO FORTY IN A HEARTBEAT

Soon after we moved into the WareHouse, we began to pray about the five acres of land immediately to the north of our site. If we were able to purchase that land, it would open up a future for our church to serve God and the community on an even greater scale. The sellers quoted us a price far beyond what we could afford. It would cost several million dollars.

For three years, we kept watching and praying. We knew we would need the property for future growth. Additional parking, a children's playground, green space, and a sports field were all dreams we had for our campus, but we thought it all impossible. However, when God is involved, you learn to never say never.

In the fall of 2013, we heard that the land was going into foreclosure. One of the men from our land and facilities team showed up for the foreclosure hearing at the courthouse and met the attorney of the estate. The attorney said he would talk with his clients, and let us know if they were interested in selling. The next week we received a call that the owners were interested, but they only wanted to sell all twenty-seven acres they owned. We asked for a price. The family who owned the land only wanted to recoup their investment, so the entire twenty-seven acres would cost just a little more than a quarter of the price that we had originally been quoted for the five acres. This was unbelievable! We drew up a contract and sent it off to the owners. We did not hear anything for a week or so, and we knew something was up. Finally, the executor of the estate called and said that one of the owners had changed her mind and no longer wanted to sell the land. The attorney and the executor deeply apologized because they felt they had misrepresented her intentions to us. We were bewildered, but we knew God was in control. He was the one making everything happen in the first place. If he wanted us to have the land, then it would happen.

After a couple of weeks, the head of our land and facilities team followed up with the executor. He told us, "You guys must have been praying because yesterday this deal was dead, dead as a door nail. Now today, the owner wants to sell, and they want to close by the end of January because they need money for a new house." We were shocked and excited at the same time.

We had only four weeks to close, and as only God can, he brought everything together. A bank stepped up, gave us a great interest rate, the appraisal came through, and all the closing documents were executed. We were able to purchase all twenty-seven acres way under market value. God grew our campus from just over twelve acres to forty acres overnight. Only God!

FROM HAITI WITH LOVE

Soon after the destructive hurricane in Haiti in 2008, we sent a team of seven people from Rolling Hills to help. We knew this would be a tough mission trip because of the tremendous needs. Because of the difficult traveling conditions, the trip kept getting pushed back. As a church, we were monitoring the situation closely and helping where we could from Tennessee. For a while, it seemed this was best. There were so many rescue organizations from around the world already on the ground and doing great work in Haiti. I am so thankful for these organizations and for the difference they made during such a horrific time.

Although our church was involved from a distance, we still felt compelled to send our team. The time finally opened up. There was an orphanage that was overwhelmed with children who had lost parents and extended family in the hurricane. Our team prepared to be the hands and feet of Christ, to care for and love the orphans of Haiti, as well as take much-needed food and supplies.

At the last moment, one of our team members got sick and could not go. Even so, a team of six decided to press on. When they arrived in Haiti, they were immediately overwhelmed at the destruction.

The team worked each day in the orphanage. Inside the gates, God was meeting the needs of the children there. Our team had brought supplies and much needed support. Outside the gates, however, civil unrest was growing. The frustration over the perceived lack of help was causing demonstrations in the streets. The orphanage directors worried that if the people outside knew Americans were inside, they might try to get in for money or food. When the situation seemed like it could not get any worse, a cholera outbreak started. People were dying and the hospitals were overrun.

The team was supposed to fly out of Haiti on a Wednesday, but the airport in Port-au-Prince was closed because of the unrest and remained closed for several days. At that point, food and supplies in the orphanage were starting to run low. No one could leave to buy more food because of the cholera outbreak, and roads were closed to any supplies being brought in because of the civil unrest.

After a week, the situation was growing desperate. Our team was growing concerned for not only the health and well-being of the children, but for their own health as well. There was little food, and the clean water supply was running low. Despite all our efforts, we could not get the airlines or the airport to tell us when they would open again. When I talked to our team members, I could hear the desperation in their voices.

As I hung up the phone, I got down on my knees to pray. "God, we need a miracle. You love the children in this orphanage, and you love our team. Please, God, provide as only you can." At that moment, God brought to mind a man that I had not talked with for a few years. I knew this man had a plane, so I gave him a call.

When Hamp answered the phone, I described the situation. He said, "I don't know if I can help, but let me see what I can do. I will call you back."

Sure enough, about five hours later, he called back. "How many people are there?"

"Only six. One team member had to stay in Tennessee."

"Good because my plane only seats six. Let me check some other things. I will call you back."

At about ten o'clock that night, Hamp called and said, "Okay, I will go get them in the morning. Just let them know I am coming."

"Awesome. Also, do you think you could stop in Florida to pick up food and supplies for the children of the orphanage?"

"You got it!" Hamp answered.

Early the next morning, Hamp took off. I still do not understand how it all came together—picking up food and supplies, landing at Port-au-Prince and paying cash to refuel (even though the airport was still closed), landing in a field by the orphanage, carrying in the food and supplies for the children, getting the team out of the orphanage and onto the plane, as well as taking off from the field while at the maximum weight limit.

I will never forget being at the Nashville airport past midnight as the small plane arrived. Family, friends, and church members celebrated the arrival of our team. We praised God for bringing them home, and we thanked Hamp for his time and sacrifice. It was truly one of those God moments. It was a miracle.

I believe all of these stories illustrate how God wants to provide us with immeasurably more than we could even dream. These stories also showcase an important aspect of our relationship with God: trust.

Doubt creeps in and threatens our faith. In bits and pieces, we wonder, "Could God really come through for me?" When we do that, what are we actually communicating to God? What are we doing to our relationship with him? If we do not trust God to stick to his word, to always be faithful, then we are questioning the very essence of God.

When we trust God to be who he says he is, we can trust God to move and perform miracles in our midst. We can trust God with our lives. We can trust him to guide our path and provide for us in ways that we don't even realize are possible.

The Israelites had to believe in a powerful and faithful God, and trust God with their lives, in order to enter the Promised Land. When Rolling Hills needed a place for our church to continue to worship the Lord and find new ways to reach our community, we had to trust God to provide. Only God could have provided for the Haitian orphans and for our team in the way that he did.

I encourage you to take a look at your own life. Are there places in your life where you need to trust God? Is it with your health or your marriage, your house or your job? Do you need to trust God with your life? Trust can make all the difference in the way we approach life.

Reflecting on these stories shows me that all too often we dream too small. We must never forget about the power of God. You see, as humans we are limited in our thinking. As God says in the book of Isaiah, "'For my thoughts are not your thoughts, neither are your ways my ways,' declares the Lord."[33] God wants to do something even greater than what we can imagine. Often, our vision is limited and we can only see one or two options when facing challenges or uncertainty. We look at what has been done before instead of looking at the unending creativity of our God. We never thought about a warehouse, but God did.

Miracles are bigger than us. That is why they are miracles. If we can do it, then we do not need God. It is when we realize our own weakness that God does what only he can do. We all face problems too big for our understanding or capabilities to solve. Think about the Israelite spies who were scared of the giants living in the Promised Land. Many times life seems overwhelming and our problems too great, yet we must always know that our God is greater! As you seek God's leading in your life, simply be open to what he can do and trust him to be the loving and gracious God that he is. Look for things outside of your normal path. Explore your dreams, even those you think would be impossible. Do not simply fall into the same path as those around you, or do what everyone says you ought to do with your life. Be open to God's possibilities. You may think, "There is no way," but don't forget about God.

MOVE OVER FOR A MIRACLE

CHAPTER 7

MIRACLES HAPPEN IN GOD'S TIMING

God's timing is always perfect. He is never late or early, always just on time. Hearing this can be incredibly difficult from our human perspective. There are times when we face trials, challenges, and uncertainties, and we wait, praying for God to move in our lives and the lives of others. We want all the answers immediately, yet God often does not work that way. His way can be progressive revelation. So we wait—and in that time we learn and grow. This causes us to stay focused on God and connected to him in prayer. We learn to walk by faith; knowing God is always a step-ahead.

Think about Lazarus. He was a guy in the Bible who was a friend of Jesus. He became sick, and his family and friends asked Jesus to help. But Jesus took his time getting to Lazarus, and before he arrived, Lazarus died. Dead. Game over. Where was Jesus when Lazarus needed him? Why hadn't he come right away?

Jesus waited before he came. Why? Maybe Jesus was operating on a different timetable than the rest of the world around him. Before even arriving in Lazarus's town of Bethany, Jesus knew Lazarus was dead. His disciples did not quite understand, "So then he told them plainly, 'Lazarus is dead, and for your sake I am glad I was not there, so that you may believe. But let us go to him.'"[34] As Jesus arrived in Bethany, both Mary and Martha, Lazarus's sisters, cried to Jesus about the death of their brother. They both wished he had been there to save Lazarus. Jesus himself was moved to tears over their pain and sadness. He asked them to take him to the tomb and remove the stone from the entrance. People wondered if this was a good idea because Lazarus had already been dead for four days. "Jesus called out in a loud voice, 'Lazarus, come out!'"[35] And here's the miracle—Lazarus actually walked out of the tomb to Jesus. Lazarus had come back to life. People did not understand the timing of Jesus's arrival, but in the end, no one questioned the miracle.

God is never late. Now, his timing is not always our timing, but his timing is always perfect to accomplish his plans. Sometimes we miss witnessing a miracle because we are not willing to wait for Jesus. We must remember that our call is to walk with Jesus every moment and leave the timing of the miracle up to him. Life events may catch you by surprise, but they do not catch God by surprise. Nothing does. God is in complete control always and forever. Many times, things that seem unexpected to us are leading us to even greater blessings in Christ.

HANNAH

In the Old Testament of the Bible, we learn about a woman named Hannah. When we meet her, Hannah is married to a man named Elkanah, and does not have any children. Infertility is a difficult struggle. Many of us have personally walked through it ourselves or know couples who have gone through infertility. It is a difficult time of trial that can test our faith.

In Hannah's day, it was no less vexing to be without children who were desperately wanted. In fact, wives in that time period had little to no status in society if they did not produce a son. Some people even looked at infertility as a sign of a curse from God. As Hannah went year after year without a child, she must have felt the eyes of everyone on her, speculating why God had not blessed her with children.

Elkanah had a second wife, Penninah, who had many children. (Back in the Old Testament, men often had multiple wives. That was a cultural trend, not one that God desired.) Can you imagine what that was like for Hannah? Not only did Hannah struggle with her unfulfilled longing to bear her own children, but she also had to live in the same house with Penninah who had all that Hannah wanted. Penninah was not very understanding toward Hannah either. When the family visited the temple each year to worship and make sacrifices to God, Penninah taunted and tormented Hannah to the point where she cried and could not even eat. Hannah must have felt incredibly alone.

One year, at the end of the meal at the temple, Hannah was incredibly distraught. With Eli the priest nearby, Hannah stood up and began crying out to the Lord:

> And she made a vow, saying, "Lord Almighty, if you will only look on your servant's misery and remember me, and not forget your servant but give her a son, then I will give him to the Lord for all the days of his life, and no razor will ever be used on his head."
>
> As she kept on praying to the Lord, Eli observed her mouth. Hannah was praying in her heart, and her lips were moving but her voice was not heard. Eli thought she was drunk and said to her, "How long are you going to stay drunk? Put away your wine."
>
> "Not so, my Lord," Hannah replied, "I am a woman who is deeply troubled. I have not been drinking wine or beer; I was pouring out my soul to the Lord. Do not take your servant for a wicked woman; I have been praying here out of my great anguish and grief."
>
> Eli answered, "Go in peace, and may the God of Israel grant you what you have asked of him."
>
> She said, "May your servant find favor in your eyes." Then she went her way and ate something, and her face was no longer downcast.[36]

I can almost hear the pain in Hannah's voice in those verses. Her cry to God is one of such anguish and despair! She loved her father God and trusted him to hear her prayer. More than that, she trusted him with her child, promising that any son she bore would be dedicated back to God.

The family returned home, and a short time later Hannah became pregnant. Praise the Lord! When the baby came, it was a son and Hannah named him Samuel. In Hebrew, Samuel sounds like "heard by God," which Hannah certainly was.

Hannah kept her promise to God, When Samuel was weaned, she took him to the temple along with an offering. Hannah took Samuel to Eli, the priest, and reminded him of her presence in the temple not long before. She presented her son to the Lord to worship God and work in the temple. As time went on, God began to show his plan for Samuel's life. He became a great prophet of the Lord, and through him God anointed both Saul and then David to become kings over Israel. God's timing of Samuel's birth was perfect.

THE CALL BACK TO CHURCH

I have been honored to see God's perfect timing play out in the lives of so many people. It is incredible to see people be drawn to Christ in his timing and for his glory. God always shows up at the perfect time.

Several years ago, I met a woman named Maureen. One of her coworkers attended our church. Each week, he would invite Maureen to church, and each week she would tell him that she did not go to church. He kept inviting, and she kept turning down his invitation. That happened over and over until one week, unbeknownst to him, Maureen showed up at Rolling Hills. She slipped into the back of the auditorium, listened, and left as soon as the service was over.

Maureen later shared her story with me. She told me about a vow she had made when she was twelve that she would never to return to church. You see, when Maureen was growing up, her mom would abuse her. When she was twelve years old, she received a terrible beating, and she ran away to the home of the local priest. The priest told Maureen that he did not want to deal with the situation, so he called her dad to come get her. That night, she received the worst beating of her life. She became angry at God and the church, so for thirty-five years, she hadn't set foot in a church.

After that first Sunday, Maureen kept coming to church. Week in and week out, she just showed up, sat there, and left as soon as the service was over. When I met Maureen, I asked her what she thought of it all. She responded, "Well, I'm not singing." "Okay," I said, "Why don't you sing?" She replied, "If I start to sing, then I feel like I will be giving in." Her heart still was not ready, but God was at work.

About one year later, I saw Maureen on a Sunday morning, and I again asked her what she thought of it all. She said, "Well, I am starting to sing." It was not long after that when Maureen gave her life to Christ. She was baptized, and it was an awesome celebration.

Thirty-five years is a long time to wait for change to take place, yet the transformation in Maureen—the way God reached out through her co-worker, her commitment to Christ, and God's great love for her—was all revealed in his timing. And the story of Maureen does not end there. She truly came alive spiritually on the day of her salvation, and she has been an important part of God's timing in the lives of other people, as well.

Not long after Maureen was baptized, she joined a small group at our church and started inviting people to Sunday morning worship services. Maureen invited her brother and his wife. When Maureen's sister-in-law, Jennifer, began coming to church, God moved in to her life too. Jennifer was working as a successful corporate attorney, but she knew there had to be more in life. She went to church when she was growing up, but had been away for a long time. Jennifer yielded her life fully to Christ and began serving in the church. The following year, Jennifer went on her first mission trip to Moldova, and her life has never been the same.

Here is one of Jennifer's Facebook posts:

I have never posted a throwback Thursday photo, and this one may not be much of a throwback given it was taken in July of 2010, but after last night's JMI Gala, I thought back to this particular moment and how God is writing my story. This photo was taken within the first ten minutes after stepping off a bus to meet my very first group of Moldovan orphans on my very first international mission trip. I remember it like it was yesterday.

Six trips later, and a ticket in hand for my seventh, this was the moment that God began preparing my heart for what He had in store for me. Though it was only three years ago, I hardly remember my life without the joy of knowing the precious children of Moldova. From the first 'please-don't-let-go-of-me' embrace from these three grimy, smelly, cavity-ridden kids, my life was changed forever. I am so very thankful for my mission-minded church family and its non-profit mission organization, JMI, that gave me the opportunity to go on that first international mission trip. One of JMI's primary missions is to change the lives of orphaned and vulnerable children through the love of Christ, and I have personally witnessed their impact for countless numbers of children. However unintentionally, the impact on a two-parented, middle-class, middle-aged professional has been no less dramatic. #Blessedbeyondmeasure.

In his timing, God drew Jennifer back to Christ, and her life has been radically transformed. From that first trip to Moldova, God has changed Jennifer's priorities and her purpose in life. She now leads mission teams to Moldova during her vacation weeks, sponsors multiple children, and continues to impact the lives of hundreds of precious orphan children with clothes, shoes, love, and support. Jennifer serves as the attorney for our Justice and Mercy International Board and is active at church every week. God is using her to change a country, yet she will tell you that she is the one who has been changed the most.

TOUGH GUY TRANSFORMED

The tools God uses in his timing are amazing to see. For Maureen and Jennifer, God was drawing them to himself through a coworker and family member, both extending an invitation to join in what God was doing. In another life, a baby girl started the wheels of change for a tough young man.

Ken and his wife, Martha, had been attending Rolling Hills for a few years, Martha more often than Ken. In fact, Ken was not always the dedicated man of God we see active in our church today. Here is a letter I received from Ken recently:

> *This is a very complicated letter for me to write as I come from an atheistic background. I went to a Catholic elementary school and was raised in a nominally Christian household, but even as a child I had an inherent distrust of the Catholic Church's authoritarian demand for unquestioning belief in the complexities of religion. I was a militant atheist by the time I reached high school, and college did little to temper my intolerance of religion.*
>
> *As soon as we graduated college, I married the only woman I ever dated, whom I met in my first class in my first semester of college. Over the course of our relationship, I'd seen the deep inner peace and steadfast faith my wife possessed, but could not relate this to my own life. In neither of our lives did church play a significant role, but she had faith where I did not.*
>
> *Once we moved to Nashville for my graduate school, we found ourselves alone for the first time in our lives. She had no family or friends nearby, and my extensive network of friends and acquaintances was thousands of miles away. Our first year was very lonely and difficult to bear.*
>
> *A year after moving to Nashville, we met another newlywed couple who introduced us to Rolling Hills. My wife quickly became involved in the children's ministry, but I was VERY reluctant to associate with any religious organization. My wife slowly convinced me to at least join her in the toddler room at the movie theater as an extra pair of hands, assuring me that there was no commitment to faith in holding a screaming baby for an hour. Since this was my first experience with very young children, I was reluctant (understandably, in my opinion) to touch these baby things. I joined my wife in this child-watching for several weeks, though I found these highly breakable little people*

VERY intimidating.

One day, a baby girl came to the ministry and could not be consoled by any of the women working in the baby or toddler areas. After all of the women had taken a turn with the girl without result, they asked me (in sheer desperation) if I could at least hold her and keep her from upsetting the other babies. As soon as she saw me, she practically jumped into my arms. The significance of this leap of faith is only realized once you recognize that I was a somewhat larger, grumpy, mohawked man in shredded jeans and a t-shirt, lounging carelessly nearby without any interest in the little people crawling around me.

I consider this moment as the beginning of my reconciliation with the church.

I had hardened my logic, intellect, and professionalism to religion through hours of study and debate, and could rebuff almost any appeal that religion could hold. All of this preparation was nothing compared to this tiny baby wanting only to be held and comforted by me in a new and confusing place.

Every week thereafter, this baby girl would arrive, and her parents would (reluctantly) give her to the only person in the room who could soothe her. Through her, my steadfast atheism and clinical skepticism was overcome with stacks of blocks and a fascination with toddler-safe toys.

Eventually, the time came when the classes were moved up. A new batch of children was introduced to Sunday school, and the baby girl became a confident student of the Lord. I wasn't sure what would happen, but of course there were more babies who would go to no one but the grumpy man with the mohawk.

Over the years, my wife and I became the sole watchers of the toddler class during first service. The mohawk eventually faded away, and I became comfortable with babies, toddlers, and young children. The children came to view my wife and I as safe people in a time when few children accept anyone but their parents in that role. This became especially important when we found that we were unable to have children naturally.

If I had not had so much experience with small children, I might not have been so keen to have children of my own, especially given the difficulty and expense associated with the procedures. Only through the support of our church family, community group, and parents were we able to finally have our own baby girl, and we look forward to many more to come, thanks to our involvement with our church family.

My wife and I have enclosed the first of many tithes to come. Though we could not pay our tithes in money while I was still in grad school, we have tried to pay our tithes in love and time. I have finally finished school, and although I will now be on the road quite a bit, I do not intend to miss a single Sunday when I can watch toddlers.

God has shown me that I have a gift for comforting small children and a gift for science. To this day, I can't decide which is the greater gift, but I intend to use both to the utmost of my abilities for my immediate family and my church family.

Thank you Rolling Hills and Jeff Simmons for allowing a disbeliever to find his own way to God through your flock.

Sincerely, from the bottom of my heart,

Ken

Wow. The change in Ken's life has been incredible. His wife, Martha, was praying for years for her husband's heart to change, for him to again find his faith. She could never have imagined that the beginning of his return to faith would come in the form of a crying baby girl. God worked in his timing, bringing together Ken and that little girl as two people who desperately needed each other in that moment.

This is the miracle of life change: God working inside of a person to transform lives for his glory. This change always happens not on our timing, but His. When God brings to life a spirit, a purpose, and a calling, it is truly unbelievable to watch! God's timing allows the changed to change the lives of others. I love seeing God change lives!

If God's miracles always come in his timing, we often find ourselves in times of waiting. We wait for God to change the hearts of our family. We wait for the miracle of a child. We wait for healing from illness. As we open our spiritual eyes and look for God's miracles, we also need to be fully present in a time of waiting. How do we do that? Romans 12:12 gives us great instruction: "Be joyful in hope, patient in affliction, faithful in prayer."

Be joyful in hope... Even in times of waiting—especially in times of waiting—we need to remember to worship the Lord. We can rejoice in the hope we have in Christ, that our belief in him is our salvation. We can also worship God for all he is doing in our lives. Look for places in your life where can you practice gratefulness.

... patient in affliction... Ah, patience. Sometimes being patient is so much easier said than done. Patience is valued by God and is outlined in the Bible as a fruit of the Spirit.[37] It would be fantastic if we were born with all of the patience we need, but do you know how patience is developed? Through trials and waiting. Use times like these to rest in God. Trust in him to hear your prayers and be patient in his timing.

...faithful in prayer. When waiting, it can be easy to feel like we have lost sight of the Lord, or that he has lost sight of us. Waiting can be lonely and difficult. But God is always with you and wants to talk with you through prayer. Are you frustrated with the wait? Tell the Lord. Are you afraid? Tell God. Like Hannah, it is okay to cry out to God, to express your pain and anguish and ask for mercy. In prayer, we recognize God is in control and we affirm our trust in him.

When you find yourself hoping and praying for a miracle, take heart. The Lord hears your prayers. His miracles always come. But remember, they always come in his timing.

I remain confident of this: I will see the goodness of the Lord in the land of the living. Wait for the Lord; be strong and take heart and wait for the Lord. Psalm 27:13-14

CHAPTER 8

Don't Miss
The Miracle

Think about the creativity of God. There are more than 123 different miracles listed in the Bible, and those miracles come in all different shapes and sizes. From God creating the world to Jesus healing a blind man, God is involved in the large and the small events of life. He is both enormous and personal all at the same time. It is amazing to think that God cares about every detail of our lives.

Some people believe that God created the world and then stepped back, essentially saying to all of us, "Good luck. You figure it out." Yet, the Bible shows us a God who is intimately involved in every detail of life. He is sovereign over all creation and yet stoops to heal an individual leper who was a social outcast—one of the lowest of the low. God sees our needs, and he meets them. No detail of our lives is too big or too small for him. He is a God of love and grace, and he is constantly at work in our lives.

Miracles occur when the supernatural invades our natural world, our circumstances, and ordinary events of life. Miracles are meant to point us to God and always occur in line with his will. Just wanting God to intervene in order to further our own agenda or to make our own names great is not what it means to seek him. Because of this, many people miss the miracles. They are looking for the blessing instead of the source of the blessing. If we open our eyes, we will begin to recognize miracles all around us.

THE MIRACLE OF MOVING A STORM

On October 23, 2015, Hurricane Patricia made landfall in southwest

Mexico. Patricia was the most intense tropical cyclone ever recorded in the Western Hemisphere, with maximum sustained winds of more than two hundred miles per hour. For several weeks, meteorologists tracked this storm. The damage was expected to be the worst in history. Everyone was worried about how many lives would be lost to this storm and how widespread the damage would be.

But according to many, a miracle happened. In a *USA Today* article on the storm, Rick Jervis wrote, "Experts say Mexico's mountains and quick mass evacuations saved lives over the weekend. But ask local residents and they say prayer played a role. 'God takes care of us,' said Yolanda Garcia Casillas, 49, who rode out the storm in this seaside community 20 miles south from where the storm made landfall."[38] Somehow and in some way, thousands of lives were saved. Call it the mountains, evacuation plans, or prayer—a miracle happened.

How many miracles does God do that we never see? Some are big and some are small. But, they happen. We live in a world that has been trashed by sin and destruction, but God is still at work. He is redeeming and restoring, and in the process, he is transforming lives.

THE MIRACLE OF A FAMILY

One of the first orphan children we met on our first mission trip to Moldova was a twelve-year-old girl named Inga. She was living at the Internat 2 orphanage in Chișinău, the capital city of Moldova. Inga's mother had been trafficked, so she had grown up without much help or much hope. Human trafficking, when humans are exploited and bought and sold especially for sex, is a large problem in Moldova. Inga was quiet, shy, and beautiful. She dreamed of having a family of her own but couldn't imagine how it could ever happen.

On that same mission trip, a woman on our team fell in love with another young girl at the orphanage named Alicia. When the woman returned to the United States, she talked with her husband about bringing Alicia to be a part of their family. Although it is difficult to bring a child from Moldova to the United States, God opened the door. This family was able to bring this thirteen-year-old girl into their home. The entire Rolling Hills community embraced Alicia, and her life was forever changed.

Soon after Alicia arrived, she began talking about her friend, Inga. This was the Inga we had first met at the orphanage. Alicia would pray for Inga, and we prayed as well. We felt like there had to be something our church in Nashville could do to help this child in Moldova. One of the original members of our clubhouse Bible study kept thinking about Inga. She and her husband had two incredible daughters. They thought they were done having children, but God had other plans for them as well as for Inga.

Through some unbelievable circumstances (that is how miracles happen), God brought Inga from Moldova to live with this family. Overcoming obstacle after obstacle, Alicia and Inga came from state-run orphanages in Moldova to be a part of families in the United States. If this was all, it would be enough. They were now safe, well fed, and clothed, but God was not finished with their story.

Alicia and Inga both became active in the Rolling Hills youth group, learning about God's word, experiencing community, and having a lot of fun. God kept working in their hearts and lives, and they were both baptized into Christ in amazing celebrations! Both Inga and Alicia graduated from high school and went on to different colleges. God truly gave them a "hope and a future."

Before we knew it, both young women were getting married. I had the privilege of officiating Inga's wedding at the Schermerhorn Symphony Center in downtown Nashville. It was an incredible evening, and we could truly feel God's presence. I stood in awe thinking about that twelve-year-old orphaned child from Moldova now being married to an amazing man in one of Nashville's most beautiful settings. This was truly God answering prayers beyond our wildest dreams.

Today, Alicia is the mom of two beautiful girls. She is active at our South Nashville campus and serves every Sunday. Inga is the mom of two precious boys. She is actively involved at our Franklin campus. Recently, Inga posted online that she was helping her children pack shoeboxes full of toys and gifts for the Operation Christmas Child program run by Samaritan's Purse. She wrote that those were the same shoeboxes that she had been so excited to receive when she lived in the orphanage. She never dreamed she would be packing a shoebox with her own children and writing notes to the kids who are in the orphanage where she once lived.

Alicia and Inga experienced miracles in their lives, and now they are making it possible for others to experience miracles as well. From their own children, to their church family, and even other orphan children, they are impacting generations with the love of Jesus Christ. They are miracles, and through them, God is doing miracles in others. They are orphans no more. This is the miracle of a family.

THE MIRACLE OF A MOMENT

One day early in the life of Rolling Hills, I received a phone call that my friend Bill had fallen and was rushed to the hospital. When I arrived there, the doctors told me that they were not sure Bill would make it. I could not believe the news. I had just seen Bill a few days earlier. How did things change so fast? I went into his room and found him hooked to every line and tube imaginable. He was in coma. I did the only thing I knew to do: pray.

I was faced with a challenge. I knew that God was inviting me to be bold and to pray for healing. Yet, what if it didn't work? I mean, what if I prayed there, in front of Bill's wife and children, and he still died? I know, I am a pastor and I should be past this, but like many of us can be, I was apprehensive. So, I stood there looking at my friend and his family and thinking about my God. What was I supposed to pray—for healing in this life or ultimate healing in the next?

The Bible clearly says, "This is the confidence we have in approaching God: that if we ask anything according to his will, he hears us." [39] The God of the universe is inviting us to ask, and in that moment, he was inviting me to ask on behalf of my friend. But I stood there in doubt. Then, it hit me;

God is sovereign. He will accomplish his will in the best way possible. He loves Bill more than anyone in that hospital room. God loves Bill's family. God could heal my friend, and we would rejoice. God could also choose to say Bill's time on earth was done, and we would give God glory because there is eternal life that waits. God won either way, so I just needed to be bold and ask. I had to push past my own worry about how I would look, and point people to the God who can and does heal.

At that moment, the Holy Spirit moved. I cannot tell you what we prayed, but we could sense the presence of God. God was in that hospital room. We prayed bold prayers, and we affirmed that God was in control. We learned to trust, to ask, and to submit to the will of God.

By God's grace, Bill was healed. The doctors could not explain his recovery but we could. He continues to be a leader at church and enjoys spending time with his family. God chose to give him more time on this earth, and Bill is making the most of it. None of us will ever fully understand what happened in that hospital room, but we definitely know that a miracle took place in that moment.

THE MIRACLE OF A MARRIAGE

I believe God wants us to have great marriages! Many people miss out on the seeing all God is doing around them because they are frustrated in their marriages. When things are out of sync at home, it is more difficult to live for God in every area of our lives. I believe marriages are under attack today because our enemy knows if he can destroy this foundation, he can keep people on the sidelines spiritually. God wants our marriages to thrive instead of just survive. He longs for us to be the husbands and wives, and fathers and mothers that he created us to be.

To succeed in our marriages, we have to invest time. It takes scheduling time with our spouse so we do not drift apart. It takes love and respect. It takes forgiveness—that is a big one. We need to always be moving forward in Christ and surrounding ourselves with godly people who are encouraging and challenging to love our spouses well. And, sometimes, it takes a miracle. Here is an email I received recently:

Hi Jeff,

My name is April[40] and I wanted to thank you for your message this past Sunday. God used every word you spoke to encourage and heal my marriage. You see, at the end of September I discovered the most devastating news about my husband. It has rocked me to the core and left every fiber of my being yearning for God and his truth. I found out that my husband is a sex addict and had been having an affair with one of my closest friends for eight months.

I love my husband and want to make our marriage work, and he feels the same, so we have been desperately seeking a church in hopes that God can bring us through this and actually turn this horrible mess into something good.

Which brings me to this past Sunday... We have made a commitment to be at church every Sunday. We feel like it's vital to our marriage, and we really want to be involved with people that will lift us up through this trial. This past weekend was particularly busy, and I kept wrestling with going to church or not. Every time the thought of skipping the service would come into my head, I pushed it away because I knew the sermon was going to be about Gomer[41] and I thought it would be important for me and Jack (my husband) to hear the story.

Saturday evening I was really sick with flu-like symptoms. Jack said we should just stay home the next day, but I refused. I thought I would be fine if I could just rest. Sunday morning, I felt horrible! I was running a fever and could barely get out of bed, but I pushed on and proceeded to get ready for church.

As I was trying to get myself and both boys ready for church I was becoming very flustered. I went to tell Jack something; he was in the bathroom with the door shut. I cracked the door to ask him a question and went on my way. As I walked away it hit me: Jack had the computer with him while he was in the bathroom all by himself. Suddenly fear rose up inside me. Was he looking at porn? Would he delete the history because he knew I would check? A million thoughts entered my mind and I decided I would just talk to him about it. I told him how it bothered me and he assured me that he was just reading the news. I was still anxious that he would do something that could cause so much temptation. He got a little defensive, so I immediately clammed up and believed the worst. Again, in that moment I wondered again what the point was of going to church. But something kept me going and I continued to get ready.

We argued the whole way to church and by the time we parked the car, I was in tears. We dropped the kids off and walked into church. We didn't speak, and my tear-stained face told the story of our morning. Through all of worship, I could barely sing; I just cried and prayed. I prayed God would save us and that he would give us strength and wisdom.

God does not disappoint! As I listened to the words you spoke I thought, "Of course, this is why our morning has been so terrible. Satan did not want us here." It was like everything you spoke that morning was just for Jack and me. By the end of the sermon, my heart was full. I had hope and felt God's love in such a powerful way. At the end of the sermon my husband leaned over, put his arm around me and simply apologized. All I could think was, "WOW, thank you, God!"

This season of my life has definitely been one of the darkest, and Rolling Hills has been a light for my family. Thank you for all you do and for being willing to hear God's voice and share it with us.

Never give up on your marriage. No matter how bad things are, there is always hope. God wants you to succeed. God wants your marriage to thrive. Go to a counselor, go to church, but first and foremost, bring your heart to God. Miracles happen, and God wants to do a miracle in you.

MIRACLES AMONG US

All of these miracles, big or small, have one thing in common: prayer. Prayer is inviting the God of all creation to invade our world and our lives. Now, God is always at work, but something happens when God's people summon him into a specific situation through prayer.

Prayer is powerful. Too often in our culture that stresses independence and pulling yourself up by your bootstraps, we forget to pray. We forget that God has invited us to call out to him. Instead, we desperately try to fix our spouse, change the behavior of our coworkers, or even correct the trajectory of our lives. There is only so much we can do alone. When we finally come to the point of giving up—giving up on our marriage, giving up on our dreams, giving up on our hope—we finally remember to pray.

I believe spiritual maturity is recognizing our weakness sooner and calling out to God immediately. Prayer changes things. Prayer is where miracles happen. Whether it is moving a storm or healing a marriage, prayer connects us with God. When writing about the prophet Elijah, James tells us, "Elijah was a human being, even as we are. He prayed earnestly that it would not rain, and it did not rain on the land for three and half years. Again he prayed, and the heavens gave rain, and the earth produced its crops."[42] I love this! Elijah was a man just like us. So many times, we think the people in the Bible were different than we are. We think they were superheroes or had some special power. But, really, they were people just like us. They prayed and God answered! It is all about God, not about them or us.

Maybe we do not see miracles because we are not praying for them. When was the last time you prayed for God to do something really big? Are you praying bold prayers for God to break into your world and do miracles? What are you praying for God to do that only he can do—not you, not someone else—only God?

Through Justice and Mercy International, I help lead a Pastors' Conference every year in the Amazon jungle. Pastors from across the region come from their villages to the community center. It takes one of the pastors nine days to come to the conference by canoe. With a team of pastors and leaders from the United States, we have a week-long conference where we teach these incredible, godly servants principles on preaching, teaching, and leadership. Most of them have never been to seminary or Bible college. They come hungry to learn and desiring to grow. Many bring their wives, and we are able to pour into and care for them as well. They sleep in hammocks and bathe in the mighty Amazon River. The fellowship is rich. Many of them are starving for godly companionship since they are serving in distant villages along the Amazon.

These men and women tell us stories of miracles. Maybe it is because there are no doctors, hospitals, or a lot of money in their villages, but the miracles they speak of are incredible. They tell us of the dead being raised, food being provided, and lives being saved. We listen in amazement. They experience God in a deeper and more dynamic way than we do in here in the United States. So often we look to doctors or money to fix a situation before we "need" God. But they immediately call out to the giver and sustainer of life, and he shows up. These people pray. They pray bold, passionate prayers. They ask for miracles, and they see God do what only he can do. As a fellow pastor friend of mine says, "We come to teach them the Bible, and they teach us about Jesus." As with most any mission trip, we go to serve, but we are the ones changed in the process.

Here's the amazing part about prayer; prayer not only changes situations and circumstances, but prayer also changes us. As we pray, we fall more in love with God. As we pray, we have a greater vision of God's work in the world. As we pray, we feel more connected to the giver of hope and life. Many times, through prayer, God changes our perspective. He invites us to trust him. God calms our hearts and minds through prayer. God brings peace into the chaos and hope to the hopeless.

How's your prayer life? What miracles are you praying for today? Maybe it is in your marriage. You feel like it is hopeless, but have you really stopped to pray about it? Maybe it is for financial provision. You feel desperate, but have you really stopped to pray about it? Maybe it is for a dream. You think it is dead because you have tried everything possible to fulfill it on your own, but have you really stopped to pray about it? Have you really wrestled with God over the entire matter? How is your prayer life?

Elijah was a man just like us. I believe the only difference between Elijah, Moses, David, and other heroes in the Bible and us today is the way that they prayed. They prayed more often and more deeply and as a result, they saw more miracles. They saw God do what only he can do. Do not wait—pray. Pray boldly and passionately. Pray big prayers and dream big dreams. Do not settle for the little that you can do on your own. Trust God and pray that He will do something great in you and through you for His glory.

Our call is to pray, and many times God invites us to be a part of the miracle. Maybe God wants to use you in the life of somebody else today. Maybe He is preparing you to be the answer to someone else's prayer.

THE MIRACLE OF HEART CHANGE

Sometimes we think, "If I just lived in Jesus's day I would get to experience all of those miracles." But, I believe God is just as active in the world today as he was back then. Jesus said, "Very truly I tell you, whoever believes in me will do the works that I have been doing and they will do even greater things than these…"[43] Inside every Christ follower, God has placed His Holy Spirit. That means you and I have power available to us—the power of the one who brings about miracles. As individuals step into their God-given potential and boldly live for Christ, then miracles happen. As people pray, God steps in and performs miracles among us.

Miracles come in all shapes and sizes. Most of the time we think about miracles on a large scale, like God sending His son to redeem mankind (the Incarnation—now that's a big miracle!). But there are also small miracles happening every day—hearts and lives that are being transformed for the glory of God. Miracles happen in hospitals, homes, and marriages in every town and on every street when we choose God over self, and His will over our own.

You see, only God can change a life. Left to our own devices, we will live lives of self-glorification and self-absorption. Without the love of Christ, we will look out for only ourselves. It is God who changes a heart. It is God who offers new life, purpose and hope. The Bible says, "Therefore, if anyone is in Christ, he is a new creation; old things have passed away; behold, all things have become new!"[44] God drawing people to himself and people coming to know Christ as their personal Lord and Savior—these are the miracles of new life. This is where hearts come alive. Then, in the move from a complacent Christian life to being fully engaged in living life for God is where hearts are transformed. People come alive and start living, investing their lives for God and in others.

Hearts and lives being transformed are actually the biggest miracles of all!

CHAPTER 9

YOUR LIFE ON
GOD'S AGENDA

Miracles are meant to move us closer to God. They reveal to us that, despite what we think and how we live, we are not in control. God is in control! Miracles call us to move from living life for our own small dreams and purposes to living our life on God's agenda. When we reorder our lives around God's plans and purposes, then we see miracles and live lives that long outlast us.

The Bible records the story of a young lawyer named Saul. He was driven, ambitious, and incredibly successful in this world. He had risen in the ranks quickly and was on the fast-track. The Jewish leadership of the day had big plans for him, and their plans were small compared to his own. He was brilliant, and coupled with his desire for leadership and power, nothing seemed to be standing in his way. His quest for success and for making a name for himself was a destiny just waiting to be fulfilled.

One day a big opportunity came. There was a growing group of people called Followers of the Way. The Jewish leaders sent him to investigate this movement and report back on what he found. All of the stir seemed to be around the rumor that Jesus (whom this guy had watched die on a cross) had come back to life. He did not believe it, but the talk was persistent. Many people were whispering about it, and the city of Jerusalem was on edge. This movement seemed to be gaining momentum and growing out of control. He would put to rest, once and for all, that Jesus was not the Messiah for which they had all been waiting.

When the young lawyer arrived, there was an argument between one of these Followers of the Way—a man named Stephen—and some of the religious leaders of the town. The argument became more heated, and the young lawyer grew angry. "Just who does this Stephen think he is?" he thought. Yet, the more he listened to Stephen, there seemed to be something different about him. There was a deeper, and somewhat beautiful, "spirit" about him. Stephen was not legalistic—firm, yes, but full of grace. Instead of evoking compassion within this young lawyer, it made him even more determined to end this movement. He wondered, "Does he think he is smarter than me? I will show him who has the power."

And with that thought, the young lawyer quietly incited the crowd, and then held their coats while they stoned Stephen. As Stephen slowly died from the injuries inflicted by one stone and then another, something was different. He did not fight back. He did not curse or struggle. He fell on his knees and prayed. He even asked God, "Lord do not hold this sin against them."[45] Then it was almost like he went to sleep. There was a peace about Stephen that this young lawyer had never seen and never known. He recognized Stephen's commitment to Jesus as he watched him die for what he believed. There was something different here, and the image was forever burned in his mind and heart.

With the death of Stephen, the young lawyer gained even more popularity and power. He was given a new title and position. With his new authority, he decided to squelch this entire Followers of the Way movement. He would take out this "church" and forever end this craziness about Jesus. It seemed like the whole city and region were catching fire, and he had to stop it now.

The man went on a rampage, raiding and arresting anyone he could find that was a Follower of the Way. He organized guards and began bursting into homes throughout the region. He was filling the jails with these followers and leading a great persecution against this church. It did not matter how many people he had to kill, he was going to win. This movement would end, and he would be the new leader of the truly religious people.

Then one day he received a report that the movement had spread to Damascus. He gathered up a small army and started on the journey. Listen to what the Bible tells us happened as he went on his way: "As he neared Damascus on his journey, suddenly a light from heaven flashed around him. He fell to the ground and heard a voice say to him, 'Saul, Saul, why do you persecute me?' 'Who are you, Lord?' Saul asked. 'I am Jesus, who you are persecuting,' he replied."[46] Saul met Jesus that day, and his life was forever changed. That miracle on the road to Damascus gave Saul a greater vision for his life than even he had imagined.

God came to him, this young ambitious lawyer who was living for the things of the world. Saul noticed how closely Jesus identified himself with the church. He had a decision to make. Saul could not live in both worlds. He had to go all in with Jesus or be totally against him. But, if he decided to go all in with Jesus, he knew that meant a giving up all that he had strived for in his life. Even so, it really was not a hard decision. Saul had now experienced what he saw in Stephen and the others. He had the peace, the purpose, and the fulfillment that he had always longed for and never found. Jesus was alive, and true life could be found in him! Everything in Saul's life was impacted by his conversion to Christ. His name was even changed, from Saul to Paul. The money, the power, and the prestige of this world did not matter to him anymore. He moved onto God's agenda and never looked back. He found the truth and became a Follower of the Way. This same man who had persecuted the church became the greatest church planter in history. He invested his life in God's work, and our world has never been the same.

YOUR LEGACY

What is your life about? Are you pursing the things of this world or the things of God? So many of us say that we want to follow God, but our lives end up looking more like the world around us than the way Christ called us to live. Our goals, dreams, and desires tend to center around worldly things instead of God's agenda. Money, power, and position can easily become the driving force for the decisions we make. We can continue to follow the way of the world, but in the end it leads to nothing. There is never enough money, power or recognition. There is never enough "stuff." The things of the world are unquenchable. It is through Christ, and Christ alone, that contentment and fulfillment come. It is only through Christ that we truly experience life. But each of us have to decide. It is an individual choice.

What legacy will you leave? When people look back at your life one day, what will they say? We would never know who Paul was if he had not moved on to God's agenda. As Jesus said, "What does it profit someone to gain the whole world and yet forfeit their soul?"[47] Paul invested his life in God's agenda—Christ and his church. Paul left a legacy of churches committed to Christ and his heart in this world, and people who were transformed by God's grace and for his glory.

As you look at your life, where are you investing? How are the people around you being impacted? Are you leading others to Christ or to yourself? Are you investing in the next generation through discipling your own kids, teaching children in church, and serving in missions? Are you leaving the world a better place than when you entered into it? This desire to leave a legacy is in all of us. Sadly, most of the time we want the legacy to be us, but any legacy like that will fade when we die. If we lead others to Jesus and move them onto his agenda, then we will have a legacy that will impact eternity.

JOHN

The idea of legacy unfolded before me above the Atlantic. I was flying to England to meet with some of our Justice and Mercy International partners to discuss a greater work for God's kingdom along the Amazon in Brazil. We gathered at the home of John Paculabo. John was the head of Kingsway Music for years. He did incredible things in that role for God: started Worship Together and Soul Survivor (introducing the world to Matt Redman, Stuart Townend, Tim Hughes, Chris Tomlin, and many more) and hosted Mission Worship and other events to grow the worship movement around the world. When I think about how the global church has been impacted through the worship music that came from Kingsway, I see how John's obedience played such a large role in drawing the hearts of thousands closer to God

About thirteen years ago, John was preparing for retirement. He and his wife had their minds set on a villa in Spain along with their home in Eastbourne, England. All that changed with one mission trip to the Amazon. While he was there, John saw a one-room building packed with children of all ages, and it was sweltering hot. He asked, "What is this?" and someone responded, "It's a school." John thought, "That's not a school."

During that first trip, John fell in love with the jungle people and became aware of their great need for Christ. John also saw a need for better education and became passionate about building schools in local villages. He and his wife forgot about the villa in Spain and began investing all their resources in mission work in the Amazon.

Over the next ten years, John helped build a million-dollar community center in the Amazon called Terra de Paz. During that time, he also helped build fourteen schools and buy a boat for teams to travel from village to village. Through Ray of Hope, a UK-based charity that John started, there is now mission work in more than forty villages along the Amazon, with countless people coming to Jesus Christ and lives being transformed for God's glory. He brought together Christ-followers throughout the world to join with him in making a difference for God's kingdom. His life is truly an incredible testimony of what God can do through one man completely dedicated to Him.

A few months before my trip over the Atlantic, John was diagnosed with stomach cancer. When I arrived in Eastbourne after my transatlantic flight that day, the nurses had just told his family that he only had a few days to live. At the airport, I joined Steve Davis, Kelly Minter, and Mary Katharine Hunt from our JMI team, and we all went to John's home. Two of John's trustees from Kingsway Trust were there, along with all of John's family—his wife, Juliet; daughter Lucy with her husband, Jorge, and their one-year-old, Savannah; his son, Joe with his wife Noelle from Brazil; and his other son Sam. John was surrounded by a lot of people who were invested with him in the Amazon. What transpired was a holy time of legacy.

When we came to the living room, John wore an oxygen mask and sat upright in his chair. He motioned for all of us to enter. We sat around him, and he asked us to pray. The people there were from three different countries and cultures, yet we were all joined in the love of Christ and the desire to see God's kingdom furthered in our world. The prayer time was deep and rich, and then John, although labored in his breathing, motioned for us to talk about the work in Brazil. He was so intent on seeing that the work would continue and grow. Although it was difficult for him to speak, John guided us to work together on a ministry that would far outlive him. For three hours, we worked, dreamed, cried, and crafted what we pray will have eternal implications in countless lives and will far outlive us all. After all of our work, John was tired and went to sleep. The next day, he opened his eyes, looked at his wife and said, "Juliet, I love you." Then he closed his eyes and went home to be with Jesus.

In John, I watched a patriarch live and die. He was an amazing man who impacted our world for Christ through worship and missions. In his last days, he surrounded himself with family and friends in order to pass on what was most important to him. We will all die. It is a fact. We do not like to think about it, but it will happen. Therefore, what matters is how we live. John's family loved him. They respected him and were blessed by him. His ministry partners loved him. Our world was changed because of his life. Now, he has heard those words that we all long to hear from the one he loved the most: "Well done, my good and faithful servant. Come and share your master's happiness!"[48]

Legacy. We do not know if we have a single day left on this planet or sixty years, but the question is this: what kind of legacy are we leaving? What are we doing each day to further God's kingdom? Are we living each day like it is our last? Let's leave a legacy that will impact others for Christ and that will far outlive us.

When we make a commitment to follow Christ, he invites us to be a part of what he is doing in the world. And because his passion is life-change, God invites us into his greater story of redemption in people's lives. When we share the love of Christ with others, God applauds, and he breathes life into them and us. We cannot change a life—that is God's job—but God wants to use us as the conduits of his love and grace. When we are open to being instruments of God, we will see miracles unfold right before our eyes!

THE FATHER & SON BOWL

Growing up, Darin did not have a good relationship with his father. Maybe you can relate, and if so, I am sorry. We all have a longing for the approval of our dad. This "father wound" impacted Darin all of his life.

When Darin and his wife, Caree, began having children, Darin resolved to be the dad that he never had. He would love his family with his words and his actions, and would support his wife and children throughout their lives. So many people end up repeating the patterns set by their parents, good or bad, but Darin resolved to change his father's pattern and his own family tree. Darin gave his life to Jesus Christ, and in God he had a Father who loved him. Darin had the approval he had always desired, and he could live in the freedom and confidence that this brings. Today, Darin is the dad of four boys, and he is a great dad!

When Darin and Caree came to Rolling Hills, they quickly became invested in our community. One day after his son's birthday party, Darin invited some dads and sons to play football. Because of his past, Darin had a God-given desire to connect dads and sons. He believed that if dads and sons could play and pray together, then a bond could form that would impact the rest of their lives. The Father & Son Bowl was born. That first Saturday afternoon was such a big success that Darin decided to do it again the next year. This time it was the Saturday before the biggest football game of the year, and more dads and sons showed up. It was a day full of fun and growth in family connections.

The Father & Son Bowl has become an annual event in Franklin. Its goal is to connect fathers and sons through prayer and football as that initial game did. At the 2016 Father & Son Bowl, there were over 1,200 players! It was incredible to see so many dads and sons playing flag football together. Kids there will tell you that this is their favorite day of the year. When asked why, they respond, "Because I get to be with my dad." In a busy world, Darin is bringing families together. Moms and siblings show up to stand on the sidelines and cheer. Some years there is snow and other years it is just cold. But, for the kids, it does not matter. This is their big game.

There are six different game times throughout the day. Before each round, Darin brings all the dads and sons into a big tent (the "Locker Room") in the middle of all the football fields. There, Darin talks to the dads about the importance of being great fathers, and then he shares his testimony. I marvel as I listen to Darin talk about not having a great relationship with his dad growing up, the change that happened in his life when he met Jesus, and his desire to be a great dad today. I see big men with tears in their eyes who commit to being great fathers and to living their lives for Christ. It is powerful!

After Darin shares his story, all of the dads and sons pray together and the Star Spangled Banner is sung. Then the music starts to pump, smoke machines go, and each team is introduced as they run out of the tunnel of smoke to their game. It is truly magical moment for these kids and dads.

Each year, Darin and Caree give a portion of the proceeds for the Father & Son Bowl to help fatherless children. The money raised helps kids in our own community through local nonprofits, as well as orphans in Moldova through Justice and Mercy International. Not only are Darin and Caree impacting the lives of children who are at the game, they are impacting children across our community and on the other side of the world!

While preparing for the 2016 Father & Son Bowl, God spoke to Caree, and she was inspired to invest even more into their event. She thought, "Why not use this event to host games for fatherless kids in our community? We can give them a chance to play with a father figure and have this incredible experience." And, that is what happened. That Sunday, there were close to two hundred players from local boys' homes and nonprofits, as well as men who stepped up from the church to play with these young men. It was called "MVP Sunday," and it was incredible! The rally tent was packed, Darin shared his testimony and God moved. With the music playing and the fields lined with people cheering, the young boys ran through the tunnel of smoke and jumped with all their heart. They are special! And, they are loved! To date, Darin and Caree have raised over $53,000 for fatherless charities through the Father & Son Bowl.

God has taken Darin's childhood experiences with his father and truly turned it into something that works for his glory. This is truly immeasurably more: Darin's life being transformed by Christ, becoming a great dad himself, and now impacting generations for the glory of our great God. God uses ordinary people to accomplish extraordinary works for him. This is what He longs to do in each of our lives. The redemption and transformation that comes in Christ is to be shared with a world in need.

Today, Darin and his own dad have had healing in their relationship. God is at work, redeeming, restoring, and making things new. God is the perfect father. We can't project onto him the failings of our own earthly dads, but we must learn to live in the confidence of a perfect father who is always there for us. From sixteen to over 1,200 players at the Father & Son Bowl today, our God specializes in doing immeasurably more.

WALKING WITH ELENA

I can't describe the emotions I felt standing in the back of that Moldovan church, with a sweet, young girl, Elena, on my arm, ready for me to walk her down the aisle. I could not fully grasp the depth of the changes God made in Elena's life since I first met her just a few short years earlier.

Let me back up. I met Elena in Moldova in 2011, when she was just sixteen years old. She grew up very poor in a Moldovan village. Her mom was sick and unable to care for her, and her father had left. Elena spent many of her early years in an orphanage. Life was hard, and she was angry, especially at her father. She even spoke of wanting to kill him.

When I met Elena, she had recently aged out of the orphanage. She had been in the hospital and she had nowhere to go. Elena's distant relative had heard of what JMI was doing in Moldova (I'm not sure how, but I'm thankful to the Holy Spirit), and shared with her about Grace House. Elena agreed to apply for the program. Honestly, she had no other options. Lisa and I heard about Elena and committed to become her sponsors through Justice and Mercy International.

When I first met Elena, she was hard. She was jaded by life and did not interact well with others. She was angry (understandably so) and hostile. But, I also sensed there was something more to her life. God was present and at work. God was drawing her to himself, and I had a front row seat to watch the process of transformation in this precious girl. She moved into Grace House and began our transitional living program there. In 2012, I had the privilege of baptizing Elena in a lake in Moldova. Since her baptism, Elena is truly a new creation. There have been bumps along the way; however, as people have nurtured her and God's word has taken root, there has been a visible, powerful change. Her life is now characterized by joy, ambition, and hope that gives glory to a God who redeems and restores.

Two summers ago, before I arrived in Moldova, Elena emailed and asked me to meet with her and a young man named Ion. Elena often emailed Lisa and me asking about advice for life, so I did not give much weight to her request. We all met at the downtown McDonald's one sunny afternoon. Ion wanted to ask advice, but he also wanted to ask for my blessing on his relationship with Elena. It was at that moment that I realized the seriousness of the conversation.

My parental instincts took over, and I began to drill him with questions. What I discovered in Ion was a man of deep faith in Christ. He loved Jesus with a full-on commitment. I found out he was teaching at a college in Moldova and working on his Ph.D. in Mathematics. I also saw his love for Elena. It was real, fresh, authentic, and deep.

Following our conversation, Elena asked me if I approved. I gave my blessing, then she asked, "Will you walk me down the aisle at my wedding?" I was honored and humbled. I had grown to love this girl as a daughter.

For the next year, I anticipated the big day. Elena and Ion planned their wedding when our Rolling Hills team would be in Moldova. It was so special that we all had become family. As I thought about my role at Elena's wedding, I was anxious about being the "father of the bride." I constantly thought about the moment, apprehensive but brimming with questions (I had never been to a Moldovan wedding), and also full of excitement. Before I knew it, I stood in the back of the church holding Elena's arm. The attendants were in place, and it was our turn to walk.

Walking Elena down the aisle was definitely a poignant moment in my life. However, it was not as emotionally gut-wrenching as I envisioned. I thought I would be a wreck. And, while I did shed tears, there was something peaceful, almost comforting, about the opportunity to walk Elena toward her future. As I placed her hand into Ion's, I felt God's presence, and I felt like my work with Elena was complete.

Now, I know I will continue to pray for and support Elena and Ion as all "parents" do, but I felt like a stage of the journey was complete, and it felt good. It felt right. To see her big, contagious smile next to Ion's steadfast, humble presence simply made me marvel at God's redemptive and beautiful plan coming to fruition. This is what it is all about as we disciple and mentor these young men and women in our transitional living programs—leading them to Christ, growing them in the faith, and helping them establish a future.

The wedding lasted seven hours (seriously, seven hours). Though it was long, the ceremony was filled with Christ. Their pastor prayed over Ion and Elena and made the ceremony personal. This was comforting as well. While I appreciated sharing, I loved the fact that they are so involved in their church that their pastor knows them by name.

Following the ceremony came the reception—and the food! Mounds of food. Tables overflowing with plates, each jam packed with delicious Moldovan creations. I loved being part of the feast, not knowing what I was eating, but enjoying it all. There was music, laughter, and even more food. For five hours, we ate. I could not help but think that this is what Jesus was referring to when he talked about the wedding feast of the lamb.

That night back in my room, I could only smile as I thought back over the day. It was so filled with joy. I think one of my favorite parts of the day was actually before any of the festivities began. There is a tradition in Moldova that when a bride leaves for her wedding, she leaves her home of origin. It was so touching to me that Elena chose to leave for the wedding from Grace House. To watch Elena, walk out of the Grace House in her wedding dress with Jazgul and Natalia (two of the young women with whom she began the Grace House program) as her bridesmaids was almost surreal. Grace House had truly become her home, and the other young women there, along with Lisa and I, had become her family. God allowed us to play a part in the way He changed Elena's life forever. What a miracle!

As a church and as JMI, we have a long way to go. There are many more kids who need our help. But, what is happening is working. Lives are being changed, and sponsors enjoy watching their kids fulfill God's plans for their lives.

I know my own time is coming. With three little girls, I imagine one day (in the very, very distant future), I will be father of the bride again. When that next time comes, I pray I have the same feeling of peace, knowing that each of my girls is in the center of God's will, marrying a man who loves Jesus even more than he loves her and who loves her so much that she keeps smiling. Yes, there will be tears. But, I pray that I experience the same feeling as that beautiful day with Elena just because I know it is right. And, maybe, this is what God felt in the Garden, where he initiated the entire "two become one flesh" idea[49]. And, just maybe that is why in creation the Father simply kept saying, "It is good!"[50]

As sponsors and as parents, God has placed Lisa and me in a position to be a part of what He is doing in the lives of some truly special young men and women. Because we trust God, He has allowed us to see some amazing life change up close, and to play a small part in his bigger story.

But parents are not the only people who can play a role in the work that God is doing in others around us. Each of us has been placed in a community for a reason. We all have people that we can reach. Take a look around. Are there people God is calling you to reach out to in your workplace? In your neighborhood? Even in the coffeehouse where you stop in a few times a week?

I urge you to pray and ask God to open your eyes, allowing you to see where you can join him in his work. Ask him to open your heart to let others in so that you can play a small part in the life change of others. The joy you will experience from seeing the transformation in someone else can't be described.

It is truly miraculous.

Section 4

BUST DOWN
THE ROADBLOCKS

CHAPTER 10

Put The Brakes
On The Status Quo

By now, you are most likely catching on to the idea that God desires for us to experience a life that is immeasurably more than we can dream or imagine, so much more than we can do on our own. So what keeps us from living that kind of life? What stands in our way? I have identified several roadblocks that can keep us from ever reaching our full potential in Christ.

They impact all of us. They are not easy to overcome, but once we do, life is never the same.

Have you ever been through a time when you were so busy that you did not have time to eat right, exercise, or get enough sleep? Do you know how you begin to feel sluggish and lethargic? You do not have the energy you used to have. You are burning the candle at both ends because of deadlines or life circumstances, but in the process you are not operating at your full potential. You are experiencing "the law of diminishing returns."

But when you push past the roadblocks of time and priorities and begin to eat right, exercise, and get enough sleep, you find there is a bounce in your step. You find that you have more energy to face the day. You find that you have a better attitude to take on the challenges before you. That is the way God designed your body to work properly.

In much the same way, unless you learn to push past the following road-blocks, your spiritual life can feel complacent. Your soul can feel lethargic. Now, I do not believe anyone responds to Christ's invitation to "Come, follow Me," and looks at it as only a "get-out-of-hell-free" card. We all want to have joy in our relationship with God and live life to the fullest. But we have an enemy who uses these roadblocks to make us sluggish in our spiritual life. Pushing through these roadblocks will help you to experience all God has for you—the immeasurably more life.

COMFORT

The first roadblock to the amazing life God desires for us is comfort. Especially in Western culture, we've designed life to make us comfortable. Air conditioning. Spas. Hot tubs. Seat warmers. We even have big, fluffy comforters on our Sleep Number beds in order for us to enjoy maximum comfort. Making comfort our goal is a huge roadblock to truly experiencing all life with God has to offer.

We like to be comfortable, but God is constantly drawing us out of our comfort zone and into His will. As followers of Christ, we are meant to be engaged in what God is doing in the world. This is not always easy or comfortable. When asked, "What is the most important commandment?" Jesus responded, "'Love the Lord your God with all your heart and with all your soul and with all your mind.' This is the first and greatest commandment. And, the second is like it: 'Love your neighbor as yourself.' All the Law and the Prophets hang on these two commandments."[51]

Loving God is not always easy or convenient. Loving God means being obedient when he calls you to do something for his name and glory. Loving God means getting up early to spend time with him, reading his word, and being actively involved in his church. Loving God means taking the time to develop a deep, intimate relationship with the one who loves you more than you can ever dream or imagine. This takes time, energy, and attention, but it is all worth it!

Loving others is not always easy either. People are messy. People make mistakes. Yet, we are called to love. We are called to be present in the struggles and to be the hands and feet of Jesus to those in need. This does not happen in the comfort of our own homes, on our big comfy couches watching Netflix all day. This happens as God prompts us to step into the mess. We respond with love, grace, and prayer at the hospital, to the neighbor, and even to the guy in the cubicle beside us. Love is not just an emotion but an action, and it very often takes us outside of our comfort zone.

In Luke 10, Jesus tells a story about a good Samaritan. Here was a guy on a trip when he saw another man who had been beaten laying on the side of the road. Now, let's be honest. Most of us would keep driving. We are in our comfortable cars with air conditioning and music playing and we have places to be. We might be like the others in the parable who passed by the man on the road—they did not want to get involved. This Samaritan? He "saw" the man.[52] Literally, God opened his eyes to the need around him. Instead of going right past the man, and acting like he did not see him, the good Samaritan stopped. He got involved. He put love into action. Again, he could have offered a lot of excuses—this man is not like me (he is a Jew and I am a Samaritan), I do not have time, I'm not a doctor, this could be a trap set up for me... and the list goes on. We have all been there. We hear of a need in our office, we see a neighbor in trouble, or we read of sex trafficking. Again we have a choice: we can stay in our comfort zone, or we can engage.

The Good Samaritan engaged. He stepped into the mess and loved his neighbor. He got off of his donkey and bandaged the man's wounds. He poured his own oil and wine on the wounded man. He put the man on his donkey (meaning he now had to walk), and he took him to a hotel and paid for his stay. The Good Samaritan loved. He did not settle for being comfortable, but he engaged and in the process saved a man's life.

Look again at the apostle Paul: in the course of his ministry, he was beaten, shipwrecked, and put in prison, all for the sake of being obedient to God and loving others. Being a follower of Christ Jesus is not always comfortable. In fact, discomfort is often where the Christian life is meant to be lived. That's right; God wants us to be uncomfortable. We do not like to face challenges, but if we don't, then we will not grow. We won't learn to trust God, follow him, and love others. We will depend on ourselves and not on God.

In the New Testament, James writes, "Consider it pure joy, my brothers and sisters, whenever you face trials of many kinds, because you know that the testing of your faith develops perseverance. Let perseverance finish its work so that you may be mature and complete, not lacking anything."[53] Many times God does his best work in the midst of our trials. We can be in the center of God's will and still go through tough times.

When you are in the midst of difficulties, hold on to God. In the tough times, look for ways to serve to others. God allows us to go through the trials, but God never leaves us alone in the middle of the storms. Our God is always doing something greater. Open your spiritual eyes to what he is trying to teach you, and ask him to use you for his glory, even in the storm.

One day, we will experience incredible comfort in heaven. But for now, we are not called to live in comfort, but to live in Christ.

With comfort comes complacency. We are in the greatest danger spiritually not when times are hard, but when times are easy. The life God is calling us to takes work, time, energy, effort, and prayer. None of those things are easy, but they all grow us deeper in our relationship with the Lord. The world will always try to make us comfortable, but that comfort can lead to entitlement and a tendency to make life about us. God wants us to trust him. He wants us to love him and love others in a way that moves us out of our comfort zone and into total dependency on him. In the process, he alone receives the glory!

IMAGE

Another roadblock to leading the life to which God is calling us is image. So often, we are consumed with what other people think. Our culture is built on image—from what we wear to what we drive. Advertisers invest billions of dollars convincing us to spend our money trying to impress people. It often seems like image is everything in our culture and society.

Getting hung up on image keeps us from experiencing the life God has for us. Because of our desire to be seen as beautiful, suave, and intelligent in the eyes of others, we become consumed by the passions of this world. Too many of us spend our time trying to figure out what to wear, shopping for what to wear, looking on Pinterest about how to wear what we are going to wear, and thumbing through catalogues and surfing the web determining what is in style to wear. We want to fit in. We want to belong.

How much time do we spend shopping online or at a mall compared to how much time we spend listening to or reading what God says about us? Of course, it is not a sin to dress nice, have a nice car, or even decorate our homes, but it is a sin when we allow any of these to become our focus or to determine our self-worth and value. When image becomes the driving force in our day, we have missed it.

God's word says, "Do not love the world or anything in the world. If anyone loves the world, love for the Father is not in them. For everything in the world—the lust of the flesh, the lust of the eyes, and the pride of life—comes not from the Father but from the world. The world and its desires pass away, but whoever does the will of God lives forever."[54]

Let's think about what is listed here. The list starts with a warning against loving the world. What does it look like when we love the world? It looks like materialism. We see "stuff", and we want it. We think having more stuff (clothes, cars, throw pillows, etc.) will make our lives easier or even make us feel better about ourselves. Sometimes our toughest decision in the day is, "What am I going to wear?" because we have so much from which to choose.

The list continues with "the lust of his eyes." What does this mean? Lust is the thought that I must have something now. So often, we think about lust in terms of sexual sin, but in reality it also applies to materialism as well. We see something we want, and we must have it now. A new pair of shoes, a new pair of jeans, a new car—anything can be a magnet for lust. It is easy for us to build on this sin by lusting after and buying things we cannot afford. We do have this little card, and we can put it on the little card, and pay for it later. The lustful thoughts of "I must have it now" are what leads to massive debt later.

All this brings us to "the pride of life." One translation of the Bible words this as "the boasting of what he has and does." This is about image. When image is king, we want our stuff to elevate us in the minds of others. We want that so badly that we are willing to go into debt or even sacrifice our relationship with God himself—the one who loves us most of all—to get it.

So we need to ask ourselves some hard questions: Do I love the world more than I love God? Am I consumed by the things of this world more than I am by the things of God? You may have an answer in your mind of how you think your heart is leaning, but how are you actually living? It is easy to find out: just look at where you spend your time and your money. Seriously. Take a time inventory and a financial inventory, and what you value will quickly become apparent. Be brave, and do this today.

Here is the heart of all of this talk about image: yes, we need clothes to wear, a house for shelter, food to eat, and we need to exist in our culture, but we cannot let the world dominate the decisions we make and determine how we feel about ourselves. If we are so busy pursuing the world that we do not have the time to spend with God each day, then our priorities are off. If we do not have any money to give to God because we are in debt from purchasing things that we feel give us status, then again we have missed the boat. We have been blessed in order to be a blessing—not simply to consume more and more stuff for ourselves.

Yes, God wants us to enjoy things. In fact, I believe God's heartbeat is for us to enjoy this life, but enjoyment comes when we are in right relationship with God first. When he is our priority in time, money, thought, and love, everything else falls into place. God does not want our leftovers. He wants to be our first thought, our first priority, our first love. That is why the very first of the Ten Commandments is, "You shall have no other gods before me."[55] If you are worshipping "the world" then this is where you will spend your time and derive your value. But, if you are worshipping God, then you will fall more in love with him.

We each are made in the image of God. This is why St. Augustine said, "Restless is our heart until it comes to rest in thee." [56] Until we discover our image in Christ, we will always be restless because finding our image in the world is a moving target. Clothes are in style, then out. Our bodies get older. We can be on top in our career for a time, then someone new comes along, or the industry changes.

Know your target. Are you living for the world or are you living for God? And, if you are living for God, then truly live for him, an audience of one. Find your worth, your value, your image in Christ, and in Christ alone.

MONEY

We don't tend to think of money as a roadblock; in fact, we often think just the opposite. We think that if we have money, then we can do miracles. But God performs the miracles and he really doesn't need us or our money.

Money, in and of itself, is not good or bad—money can be *used* for good or bad. There are a lot of wealthy people who have done great things with money. Praise God for generous disciples! I believe we are most like God when we give.

The Bible does say, "For the love of money is a root of all kinds of evil."[57] Money is not always a roadblock to living life for God, but the love of money can easily become one. Jesus said, "No one can serve two masters. Either you will hate the one and love the other, or you will be devoted to one and despise the other. You cannot serve both God and money."[58] Read that again—Jesus told us straight out, "you cannot serve both God and money," but we sure do try. We believe that money will solve all of our problems. We put our faith in money. We trust money to get us what we want. But where does our money come from? God gives us money in order to meet our needs.

Money comes with several challenges. If we do not learn to manage it, then we often find ourselves in debt. Living for money can convince us there is never enough, and we can find ourselves living as slaves to money instead of living in freedom with God. Debt keeps us from being able to answer God when he asks us to give and be generous. Let me illustrate: God prompts your heart to help a neighbor in need, and you say, "I can't. I don't have the money." God invites you to go on a mission trip, and you say, "I can't. I am in too much debt." God stirs your heart to sponsor an orphan child, and you say, "I can't. I just can't afford it." Debt keeps us from experiencing the life that God has in store for us. Now, we cannot do everything, but when God opens our eyes to see a need, he wants us to be in a position to respond. If we often find that we cannot follow God's lead in responding to the needs he shows us, our security and trust may be in money and not in him.

There is good news! When it comes to money, God says, "Test me." Seriously, God says, "Trust me. I got this!" In Malachi 3, we read, "'Will a mere mortal rob God? Yet you rob me.' But you ask, 'How are we robbing you?' 'In tithes and offerings. You are under a curse—your whole nation—because you are robbing me. Bring the whole tithe into the storehouse, that there may be food in my house. Test me in this,' says the Lord Almighty, 'and see if I will not throw open the floodgates of heaven and pour out so much blessing that there will not be room enough to store it.'"[59] Now, that is the immeasurably more life—not room enough for it all! God wants you to experience financial freedom by honoring him with the money he has blessed you with and trusting him to provide.

Maybe you are thinking, "No way. You have no idea how much debt I have built up! This is impossible." It is possible to drop your dependence on money and trust God. Look what happened in a recent Financial Peace University[60] class at Rolling Hills. Here are the results from just fifteen households:

In nine weeks the group:
- Paid off $75,535.44 in non-mortgage debt
- Saved $22,220
- Cut up or closed 63 credit cards
- 47 percent of the group remarked that they are giving substantially more as a result

Seriously! Look at this. It is possible. God can deliver you out of debt and into financial freedom. Don't be overwhelmed, but do something about it. Whether it is simply taking control of your spending or enrolling in a class like Financial Peace University, it is possible.

The challenge with money is not about how much you make, but what you do with what you make. A high percentage of professional athletes, who sign multimillion dollar contracts, are in financial crisis just a few years after leaving their sport. They had a lot of money but did not manage it well.

A simple way to overcome this money roadblock is the 10/10/80 principle. The first ten percent of what you make, you give. Biblically, this is called a tithe. This is what Malachi was talking about. Give back to God. Invest in his kingdom. Do this first. If you wait until the end of the month, the money won't be there. Plus, giving to God first demonstrates your faith in him. The second 10 percent is what you save. This is so important. Open a savings account. Put money into your retirement. Start a college fund. Do something to save some money. You will be shocked at how quickly this will add up. Finally, you live on the 80 percent. This will enable you to live below your means. If you do this, I guarantee you will bust through this roadblock. You will experience joy in the journey like never before because money will not be controlling you!

BUSYNESS

If you ask someone, "How are you doing?", most of the time you hear, "I am so busy." We wear busyness as a status symbol, a badge of honor. Busyness is one of the most common and subtlest roadblocks to our life with God. There is a difference between activity and accomplishment. We can have a lot of activity, but at the end of the day are we really succeeding at what God intends for us?

One of the biggest dangers in life is succeeding at the wrong thing— knowing God has this awesome plan for you and yet being so busy that you miss it. No one really wants to succeed in their to-do list, but fail at what really matters. There is no one to blame for our misaligned priorities but ourselves. No one is demanding that we do all the things we do except us. Parents give in to the unrealistic pressure to have our kids in every sport or activity. We know it's unrealistic but we do not want them to miss out, so we sign them up anyway. Adults sense that we, too, must be busy in order to feel like we are moving forward with our lives. So we run around like mad men and women, rushing kids from school to sports to gymnastics to dance, while we try to meet our work demands, go to parties, cheer for football games, and more. Then, we add family trips, holidays, and that small thing known as sleep, and we find ourselves quite, well, busy. Incredibly so.

The Bible invites us to, "Be still and know that I am God."[61] But in this day and age, who has time to "be still?" There is too much to do. So instead of spending time with God each morning in prayer and reading his word, or just being quiet in his presence, we jump out of bed, grab some liquid caffeine, and run out the door. Here we go living life in fast forward.

Sometimes I wonder if we keep moving so that we do not have to stop and "be still" with God. Being still requires honesty and authenticity. Maybe we are afraid to be real with God, so if we keep busy then we do not have to spend time with him. Maybe we don't want to be truly real with him or with others.

In our busyness, we miss out on what life is really about. We miss the depth of love that God invites us to experience. We miss seeing him at work in our lives, as well as in the lives of others. We miss deep, authentic relationships with our spouses and even our children. We miss the goodness of relationships with others at church, in our neighborhood, and community. Other cultures measure time by relationships, but we measure time by activity. Maybe that is why we have so few real friendships. Maybe that is why so few marriages are really succeeding. Maybe that is why, despite the activity, we really feel lonely.

Through all of our busyness, it is not only us who suffer. We take our kids with us, teaching them that a busyness is normal. As much as I love sports, I think they can be the biggest detriment to the family that our world has ever seen. We have kids in travel leagues at the age of six. Really? We buy into a lie that if our kids are not playing a specialized sport by six or seven, then they will not get a scholarship. Is this the life we want for our kids—one that idolizes sports achievements? Looking at the activity levels of so many families today, it sure seems like it. With the time we spend watching, worshiping, and investing in sports, we send the message to our kids that sports are our top priority.

If your kids know more about football or players on collegiate or professional teams than they do about Jesus, then they have missed it. And, ultimately, you have missed it as a parent. This is your responsibility. You set the schedule for your family. You make the decision what your priorities are going to be. No one else but you. Sports, dance, and all extracurricular activities are supposed to be fun, not worshipped. Kids should have fun playing on teams with their friends, not see it as a business. None of this impacts eternity. God does not care who wins the football game (although many people pray to him for their team), God cares about people. God wants the people to know his son and for their lives to be transformed for his glory!

Do you know what your kids really want?

You.

They want to spend time with you, not just driving from one activity to the next. They do not want more stuff; they want you. They want to hear your heart. They want to know what really matters to you. They want to know what you believe about God and life. They want to feel love and to share their love with you. Time together creates security.

In order to see God, you have to take control of your schedule. You cannot let activity and busyness dictate your life. You have to schedule the things that are important to you—time with the Lord, time with your spouse, time with your kids. Time is the most precious commodity you have. Set your priorities first, and then let the other activities fall where they may. Schedule time with God; put it on your calendar. Schedule time with your spouse—not just time in front of the television together, but actual date nights. Schedule time with your kids in the form of family dinners, game nights, or other activities that you can all enjoy together. Do not just be busy, be intentional with your time.

Now, when someone asks you, "How are you doing?" Instead of responding, "I am so busy," you can say, "I am grateful," or "I am enjoying life." You will see God in his word, in your marriage, and in your kids. Your life will come alive. You will understand what really matters and you will invest your time accordingly. You will discover what it means to be fully known and fully loved. You will live a life in which God is doing immeasurably more.

CHAPTER 11

HE IS FOR YOU, IN YOU, AND WITH YOU

Pushing through roadblocks becomes a matter of believing God. Remember, as the angel said to a scared young woman who was going to be the mother of Jesus, "For nothing shall be impossible with God."[62] God can and will do anything, and he wants you to succeed. He is for you! He did not create failure. His desire is that you experience all of his goodness.

We have an enemy who puts roadblocks in our way, but we have a Savior who is greater. The bottom line is this: whom or what are we going to trust? Our call is to believe God, push past the roadblocks and embrace the life we were meant to live.

FEAR

Fear is a huge roadblock. In fact, it could be said that we live in a world of fear. From terrorists to financial crises, our world is full of things that cause us to live our lives afraid. Fear consumes most people. It keeps us from experiencing the goodness and grace of God in our lives and from sharing him with others. Yet the Bible tells us, "God did has not given us a spirit of fear, but of power and of love and of a sound mind."[63]

Fear paralyzes us. Fear keeps us in place instead of embracing all God has for us. The amazing life God has for us awaits, but we are afraid to step up and step out. So many fears seem to whisper in our ears—fear of what others will think, fear of missing out on what the world has to offer, fear of dangers in this world, fear of not knowing whether God will really come through. You name it, and we can find a reason to be afraid.

Fear does not just plague us. According to an article in *The Report*

Newsmagazine, "ordinary children today are more fearful than psychiatric patients were in the 1950s."[64] Kids are growing up afraid. Anxiety is on the rise in children and adults alike. Also on the rise is the use of prescription drugs to cope with our fears. We live in fear, yet so much of what we fear never comes to fruition. God calls us to trust him and to be brave.

Even Jesus's own disciples struggled with this roadblock of fear. In Matthew 14, Jesus came to the disciples in the midst of a storm, walking out on the water to meet their waterlogged boat. The disciple Peter looked up, saw Jesus, and realized that he would be safer with Jesus on the water than without him in the boat. Jesus told Peter to come, and Peter actually did it. Peter walked on water. Talk about the immeasurably more life! But, then what happened? Peter became afraid. In fact, the Bible says, "But when he saw the wind, he was afraid..."[65] Peter took his eyes off of Jesus and began looking at the waves around him, recognizing his worry and fear. The passage continues, "...beginning to sink, (Peter) cried out, 'Lord, save me!'" Now, can you see the wind? No. Can you see worry? Can you see fear? No, but they can sink us just as they did Peter.

This story is such a great one to embrace in the face of fear. I love this truth that Jesus comes to us in the middle of storms. It is comforting to see that in the midst of his fear, Peter called out to Jesus. In the midst of sinking, he called out to the only one who could save him. And, Jesus did. "Immediately Jesus reached out his hand and caught him."[66] Notice that word "immediately." As soon as Peter called out in total need and dependence, Jesus responded.

Please understand, God does not want you to live in fear. Fear is a choice we make. We choose fear over faith. We focus on the wind and take our eyes off Jesus when what we need to do is stay focused on him and his love for us and let those fears fall away.

In the Old Testament, there was a guy named Joshua. Moses, the great leader of God's people, had died. Joshua would be stepping in to lead Israel. I have to believe that Joshua was scared. Moses, this man who had been with God face to face and had led for decades, was gone. Joshua probably felt alone. Maybe you have been there. A mom or dad passes away. What do you do? A spouse leaves you. Where do you go for help? You are afraid. But listen to what God says to Joshua in the midst of his fear: "Have I not commanded you? Be strong and courageous. Do not be afraid; do not be discouraged, for the Lord your God will be with you wherever you go."[67] Joshua embraced those words, trusted God, and was a great leader for the Israelite people. What will you be able to do as you let go of your fear and trust in the Lord?

I will never forget being at the pool with my daughter Mabry when she was little. Mabry was standing on the side of the pool with her little floaties on. I was in the water, and I invited Mabry to jump off the side of the pool and into my arms. She just looked at me and shook her head "No." "Come on!" I told her, "It will be fun!" But, all I received was the same shaking of the head—"No." And there she stood —wanting to jump, but afraid. It took her forever to decide if she was going to jump. She looked at the water. She looked back at me. She looked at the water. She looked back at me. And, then she finally jumped. With reckless abandon, she jumped with her arms outstretched and she flew through the air to land in my arms. Almost as soon as I caught her, Mabry held on to my shoulders, looked up into my eyes, and said, "Let's do it again, Daddy!"

Are you living in fear or are you living in faith?

Is your focus on Christ or on your circumstances?

Are you standing on the side of the pool or are you ready to jump with joy into the arms of your heavenly father?

God says, "Don't forget about me. I am with you!" We overcome this roadblock of fear by focusing on God. We remember that he is for us, and as God's word says, "If God is for us, then who can be against us?"[68]

The Bible tells us that, "Perfect love drives out fear."[69] You overcome fear by looking into the eyes of Christ and understanding his incredible love for you. As you focus on Christ, fear begins to disappear. You understand that he is control. He is sovereign over all creation, and he has you in the palm of his hands. When you truly internalize this amazing truth, your heart calms down and you find a life of faith, not fear, as you rest in the truth that God will "never leave you or forsake you."[70] He is with you, and he is for you! What is God calling you to do? At some point, you have to push past the fear and jump!

DOUBT

There are times when we can feel surrounded by questions, wonder, and doubts. Most of us do not doubt the existence of God (we know there has to be someone bigger than us), but many times we doubt that this God will come through in our own lives. Through worry, concern, anxiety, and fear, we express our doubt. Does God really see what is happening in my life? And, if he does see, then why does he not do something about it?

Doubt is nothing new for Christ-followers. John the Baptist struggled with doubt[71], as did Jesus's own disciples. Remember Thomas? After Jesus conquered death, Thomas made that infamous statement, "Unless I see the nail marks in his hands and put my finger where the nails were, and put my hand into his side, I will not believe."[72] Thomas is labeled as "Doubting Thomas," but truth be told, how many of us would have thought the same thing?

In her article in the *New York Times*, columnist Julia Baird shares about the Archbishop of Canterbury, the leader of eighty million Anglicans worldwide. When asked if he harbored doubts, the archbishop replied, "It is a really good question...The other day I was praying over something as I was running, and I ended up saying to God, 'Look, this is all very well, but isn't it about time you did something, if you're there?' Which is probably not what the Archbishop of Canterbury should say."[73] Even Mother Teresa commented in her diaries that she struggled with doubt.

Doubt is not a sin. In fact, doubt becomes the seedbed of faith. Doubt is not the opposite of faith; that is unbelief. There is a reason it is called "faith." Faith implies that we do not have everything figured out. Our finite brains cannot handle all the knowledge in the universe, therefore we have to believe in something or someone. Faith is a decision. It is a commitment we make. It is a stake we put in the ground, a banner we wave and cling to in the midst of the storms.

So, what causes doubts in our life? Doubt arises when things do not go our way. When God does not respond like we want him to, then we wonder and we doubt. Doubt can also come when things do not happen in our timing. We pray about something, and the answer seems to take forever to come. "Why am I still single?" "Why don't I have children yet?" "Why am I still in this job?" When our timing is not in line with God's timing, then we doubt that God cares or hears our prayers. Doubt comes when we forget all the ways God has come through in our lives in the past. We lose our perspective and our gratitude.

God can handle our doubts, questions, worries and fears. We must learn that our faith is in him, not in our circumstances or even his blessings. He becomes our rock and our refuge. As Julia Baird wrote in that New York Times article, "Just as courage is persisting in the face of fear, so faith is persisting in the presence of doubt."[74]

In Mark 9, we read about a man who brought his sick son to Jesus's disciples and asked them to heal him. When Jesus came on the scene, the disciples had been unsuccessful. "Jesus asked the boy's father, 'How long has he been like this?' 'From childhood,' he answered, 'It has often thrown him into fire or water to kill him. But if you can do anything, take pity on us and help us.'"[75] How often do we pray like this? Not boldly, but sheepishly. "If you can, God, then help me in this situation."

"'If you can?' said Jesus, 'Everything is possible for the one who believes.'"[76] Now, that is a powerful statement for all of us. Do we boldly pray with confidence in our God? If you were to examine your prayer life, what would you find? What are you boldly asking God to do in your life, or in the life of someone you love?

"Immediately the boy's father exclaimed, 'I do believe; help me overcome my unbelief!'"[77] First, I love this dad's honesty. He is growing in his faith, and he is sincere about where he is. Second, I love that he asked Jesus to help him overcome his unbelief. When we have doubts, we should pray.

The temptation is to stop talking to God until we have all of our answers, but we need to keep pressing forward, being honest and authentic with him. Remember, God can handle it. I also love that Jesus does not become angry or frustrated with this dad, but he responds in love and grace. Jesus always meets us in our honesty and in our willingness to grow. Then Jesus heals his son. The man, even in his doubts, sees Jesus do a miracle!

When God first called us to start Rolling Hills Community Church, I had so many fears and doubts. When my boss asked me how I would support my family, his question scared me to death. After our first meeting in the apartment clubhouse, Lisa and I had planned to go away for the weekend. It had been an incredibly emotional year of praying for God's will, saying goodbye to people we love, physically finishing a season of ministry, starting a new one, and moving. We needed a couple of days away, and I needed some time with the Lord.

We went to a beautiful cabin in the Smoky Mountains that overlooked a stream. On the first full day we were away, I walked beside that stream and prayed for hours. I asked God if he was sure this is what I was supposed to be doing. Obviously, I still had a few doubts. I prayed Philippians 4:6-7 over and over again: "Do not be anxious about anything, but in every situation, by prayer and petition, with thanksgiving, present your requests to God. And the peace of God, which transcends all understanding, will guard your hearts and your minds in Christ Jesus." I knew God was inviting me to be a part of his bigger story, but I was worried and afraid.

Something amazing happened by that river that day. It was not that all my questions were answered. God did not send a piece of paper down from heaven with the perfect step-by-step process outlining what I should do, but he did overwhelm me with his presence. His calm assurance flooded my soul. I felt him saying that this was his idea and just to trust him. When I walked away from that river, I was confident knowing that this was his plan and purpose for my life. I knew it would not be easy, but just knowing I was in the center of his will made all the difference. I walked away from that river and never looked back.

God always comes through. Our call is to "live by faith and not by sight,"[78] and to trust that God is doing a greater work than we can see or imagine. We must hold on, trust, and believe. In this process of praying and holding on, our faith grows. We move past the layer of doubt and draw deeper in our love for Christ. The doubts will come, and when they do, our response should be to open our spiritual eyes to a Savior who is holding his nail-pierced hands out to us. He loves us, and he invites us to come to him, even through our doubts.

There comes a point where we must lay aside our doubts and believe. As Jesus told Thomas while he stuck his fingers into the holes in Jesus's hands, "Stop doubting and believe."[79] Jesus met Thomas in his doubts, and Jesus comes to you and me as well. Jesus did not reprimand Thomas for his doubt, nor does he reprimand us for ours, but he moves us toward faith. Doubt and worries make us unstable. They keep us up at night. We toss and turn because of our worries. Yet, Jesus comes and brings peace. In fact, "Peace be with you!" is the first thing he said to his disciples when he appeared to them after his resurrection.[80]

Peace comes when we trust and believe in God. Do you have this peace today? What are your doubts? What keeps you from going forward in Christ? God wants to do great things in your life. Stop doubting and believe.

YOUR PAST

A past. We all have one. The things we have done that we forever regret. We cannot change the past, but we can learn from it. We can go forward into the future with a new hope and a new life.

People tend to live in the prisons of their pasts. Have you ever noticed that anytime you get serious about following God, Satan immediately brings up your past? "God can't use you. Do you remember what you did as a kid, in high school, in college? Do you remember what happened in your marriage? Do remember that mistake you made?" Immediately, our head drops. We remember, don't we? We remember that night, that relationship, that failure. And even though we have prayed about it and asked God to forgive us, we have never forgiven ourselves.

The past can be a major roadblock to get through on the way to a life lived for God. But there is good news: God loves to redeem our past. He loves to make all things new. With God, it is "forgive and forget." Too many people think that when we die, we will stand before God and he will have a giant video screen playing clip after clip of our past mistakes. He will run through those, like we do searching for a Netflix movie, and pick a few clips for all to see. This is a lie from Satan. In truth, if we have truly confessed our sins, then God has already forgiven us and moved on.

Now, unrepentant sin does keep us from experiencing all God has for us. If we are doing things that we know are wrong and out of line with God's will for us, then we must stop and confess. Sometimes we treat sin like it is no big deal, but our sin took Jesus to the cross. So if we are in the midst of an emotional affair, alcoholism, gambling addiction, pornography, or any other sin we will not let go, we must stop and confess. We will never experience the amazing life God has for us if we are living in unrepentant sin.

The Bible says, "If we confess our sins, he is faithful and just and will forgive us our sins and purify us from all unrighteousness."[81] This is awesome news! We confess, and God forgives. God knew that we would make mistakes in the journey, and he made a way for us to be forgiven, redeemed, and restored through our salvation in Christ. Once we confess something, we have to let it go. The Bible says, "…as far as the east is from the west, so far has he removed our transgressions from us,"[82] and that he "…will remember their sins no more."[83] This is the amazing forgiveness and grace of our God.

Just ask a man named David. This guy really blew it. David grew up loving God. He worshipped God and had a special relationship with him. God blessed David. He became the king of Israel. God was with him, and everything David did was a success. Then came the temptation.

One night David was on his roof and saw a beautiful woman bathing. Instead of walking away, David stared. Temptation is not a sin, but it can lead to sin. David could have stopped, but he blew right through the warnings and sent his servants to bring the beautiful woman to his palace. David had a one-night stand with Bathsheba and then sent her home. No big deal, right? Well, it was a big deal to God, and it became a big deal to David when word came back that Bathsheba was pregnant.

Instead of stopping the whole fiasco and confessing his sin, David tried to cover it up. He had her husband Uriah (one of David's own soldiers who was fighting in battle for him, the king) come home. David thought, "He will sleep with his wife, and then he will think the child is his." But, David's plan did not work because Uriah was loyal to his men and slept outside as they did. Finally, in an attempt to get rid of him, David sent a note to put Uriah on the front lines of the battle, and Uriah was killed. Then David, pretending to be a great guy, took Bathsheba in to be his wife and protect her. Now she could have the baby and everything was fine. But, sin is never fine with God.

God confronted David through a prophet. David had committed adultery and murder, and he needed to confess. David faced a choice. He knew there would be consequences for his sin, but he wanted even more to be in a solid relationship with God. Because David confessed, he experienced God's grace and forgiveness. David was able to see God perform even more miracles, and the rest of his years were some of his best. David is known as a man after God's heart.[84] He was not defined by his sin, but by his God.

Do not let your past keep you from knowing that God still wants to do incredible things in your life. Our God is greater than your past or your sin. He is not simply a God of the past, but a God of the present and the future. He loves to take the broken parts of our lives and redeem them for his glory. Next time Satan tells you, "You can't because of your past," you just tell him, "I can because I am forgiven." You must forgive yourself and move on. You may still have to deal with consequences, but you can live in grace and not guilt. Are you living in grace or in guilt today?

The rest of your life can be your best! You still have breath in your lungs for a reason. God is not finished with you. God wants to use you for his glory.

Do not let your past define you, but let God define you. Find your worth and your value in him. God loves you. He has forgiven you, redeemed, and restored you. Go forward in his grace, and live in the confidence of his love.

CHAPTER 12

WHAT IF THE MIRACLE DOESN'T COME?

I remember walking with a good friend through a tough season of his life. His job was in flux and his grandmother was very ill. She had cancer, and the prognosis was not good. My friend was convinced that God was going to heal his grandmother and restore her good health. He was praying for a miracle and asking all of his friends to pray for a miracle as well. He was convinced that God would heal her. However, I could not help but think, what if God doesn't? How would my friend respond?

What if the miracle does not come?

This is a question that digs at the heart of every believer. What if? What if all we desperately hope and pray for never happens? What if? What if the divorce still goes through, the house still goes into foreclosure, or the loved one still dies?

What do we do when we seem to have missed out on the miracle we are aching for?

CLING TO TRUTH

We have all been there and know others who have faced severe disappointments. Christians of all ages and backgrounds face situations when they pray for miracles that do not seem to come. It can be devastating. In times of darkness and confusion, it is easy to wonder what we should do, and we look around for something to hold on to. What should we conclude about God when our prayers appear to go unanswered?

As Christ-followers, we have hope in all situations through the love of God and the grace of Jesus Christ. Although it is easy to feel like nothing can make things better, our God is here for us and loves us. When we question God's plan and feel like we missed a needed miracle, it's time to dive deeper into our relationship with God, to root ourselves in our faith.

First, we must understand that God is Sovereign. We can hold on to the strength of a Father God who is in control. This is not an easy answer or a cop out; this is truth. The Bible tells us in 1 Chronicles:

> *Yours, O Lord, is the greatness and the power and the glory and the majesty and the splendor, for everything in heaven and earth is yours. Yours, Lord, is the kingdom; you are exalted as head above all. Wealth and honor come from you; you are the ruler of all things. In your hands are strength and power to exalt and give strength to all.*[85]

God knows more than we do. God is in control of all, from the mountains and trees, to the tiniest atoms. Take comfort in this, that God truly knows what we need. He is sovereign over all creation, and he is sovereign over our lives.

We will all experience things that we do not understand, both good and bad. In times when the miracle does not come, we can find ourselves asking God, "Why?" God is okay with our questions and glad that we are coming to him with our hurt and doubt. But we also need to get comfortable with the reality that there are going to be things in this life that we do not understand simply because we are not God. We are human beings, with human failings and human understandings. God has an understanding and perspective of things that we will never be able to grasp. We can trust in the God who rules over all.

At some of the most difficult points in our lives, we can see God do his greatest work. These are also the times when our faith can grow the most. God can redeem even the darkest situations. It is hard to perceive that redemptive power when we are in the thick of the battle, but looking back, we can often see where God moved on our behalf.

Dave, a member of our church at Rolling Hills, was in his early fifties when he went to the doctor to discuss some physical problems he was experiencing. He was a runner and in great shape. After a series of several misdiagnoses, he was sent to a specialist for a series of tests. The tests revealed a tumor in his bladder, and surgery was performed to remove the tumor.. Dave and his wife prayed, "God, please let this be nothing."

After the surgery, the tumor biopsy showed what Dave had feared the most: cancer. This healthy, successful, active, Christ-follower was now fighting the battle of his life with bladder cancer. The questions began to flow. God, why did you let this happen? God, why didn't you answer our prayers? God, how are you going to protect me and my family through this?

The twenty-seven rounds of treatment were a physical and spiritual struggle. After three and a half years, Dave's body was worn down but his spirit was lifted by the prayers of his family, friends, community group, and church. Through it all, Dave stayed faithful. Although he did not fully understand, he knew God was with him and that in the end, God had a bigger plan and purpose. Dave was not afraid to bring his questions and frustrations before the Lord, but he also trusted in the sovereignty of God.

Four years after his diagnosis, Dave was declared cancer-free. Although the fight was the hardest thing Dave had ever faced, he will tell you that he is thankful. While he was not joyful to have had cancer or to endure many years of treatment, he found joy in the midst of it and would not trade the spiritual experience that came along with it. He truly believes God has received glory in the midst of his cancer. In addition to the growth in Dave's own life, his story has had a spiritual impact in the life of countless others as well.

It was amazing to walk with Dave through cancer and to see God work in him as well as through him. He is a deeper, more committed and more faithful disciple of Christ today than before and his experience has given him the opportunity to minister to many others experiencing the trials of cancer.

When we think we missed out on a miracle, **we must realize that God is not finished with our story yet.** Just because the miracle we are hoping for has not happened does not mean that it won't. God is still writing our stories, and he is not finished with any of us. We are still alive on this earth for a reason and a purpose.

Many passages in the Bible point us to a God who is actively working in our lives. In a letter to one of the early churches, leaders Paul and Timothy wrote these encouraging words: "He who began a good work in you will carry it on to completion until the day of Christ Jesus."[86] God is at work, even if we can't see it now. His timeline goes far beyond our lives—it continues until the day that Jesus returns and beyond.

So many people give up before the miracle ever has a chance to take place. God is preparing us, but God is also preparing the situation. As I have said over and over again, God's timing is not our timing. It is so important that we understand this—that we not give up on God or on our purpose in this life. What can we do instead? We continue to pray. We must pray for peace in our circumstances, for guidance moving forward, and for trust in the Lord. Never give up!

Finally, in the midst of doubt, the question becomes, "Do we trust God?" Is he enough for us—miracle or no miracle? Can we trust him in the good times as well as in the tough times? Do we love God or just his blessings?

Miracles are not the end all be all of life. In fact, miracles are meant to lead us to God. Knowing God and growing in him is what life is about. Sometimes God allows us to walk through difficult times not only to grow our faith in him, but to expand our ministry to others. Even though we love God and follow him, we are not immune to struggles in this world. If we were, then who would model Christ in the difficulties? Who would show others how to be strong in the suffering? If Jesus himself went through struggles and trials, then why would we think we would not?

We need to trust that God is who he says he is. Throughout scripture, God tells us that he is faithful and loving. He entered into a covenant with Abraham to make his descendants more numerous than the stars in the sky, and God remained faithful to that promise. In fact, he never breaks a promise. Through Christ, God has entered into a covenant relationship with you. Do you believe what he says? Do you trust him with your life?

In the Book of Job, we read about a man whose faith was tested to the very breaking point. Job was a strong, dedicated follower of God, but he still went through difficulties. He lost his family, his health, and all his earthly possessions. In spite of all of his pain, and while he prayed for miracles with prayers that seemed to go unanswered, Job said of his own faith journey, "The Lord gave and the Lord has taken away; may the name of the Lord be praised."[87] Job's own wife told him to curse God and die, and yet he responded, "Shall we accept good from God, and not trouble?"[88] In spite of all of his suffering, in spite of the miracles that did not come, Job trusted God and believed in his greatness and sovereignty.

Job trusted God in both the good and the challenging times. Just like Job, we live in a fallen world. It is broken because of sin. We will go through difficulties, but our faith and trust is not in money, possessions, power, or things in this world that will not last. Our trust is in the one who is greater. There is a bigger picture at play, and our call is to trust God and be faithful. In Habakkuk 3:17-1, the Bible reads,

Though the fig tree does not bud and there are no grapes on the vines, though the olive crop fails and the fields produce no food, though there are no sheep in the pen and no cattle in the stalls, yet I will rejoice in the Lord, I will be joyful in God my Savior.

Our call is to trust God regardless of our circumstances. We know our eternity is secure and that God is at work in our lives every day. We must never forget his promises, and we must trust him more each day.

I continue to think about a verse in Proverbs that I memorized as a child. It is amazing how I have held on to it tightly in times of uncertainty and doubt: "Trust in the Lord with all your heart and lean not on your own understanding. In all your ways acknowledge him, and he will make your paths straight."[89] In times of worry and pain, we can rest in the arms of a God we can trust with our lives. Our God is faithful to us, and he asks us to be faithful to him. Do you trust God with all your heart?

JOY IN THE TRIALS?

James writes, "Consider it pure joy, my brothers and sisters, whenever you face trials of many kinds, because you know that the testing of your faith develops perseverance. Let perseverance finish its work so that you may be mature and complete, not lacking anything."[90] Scripture shows that there is a direct correlation between the trials we go through and our spiritual depth. I must be honest and tell you that I am not to the point where I am praying for more trials, but I do recognize that I have grown the most spiritually in those times when things were difficult. It is in those times that I prayed like crazy and held on to God tightly. Some of the godliest people I know are people who have been through incredibly tough times in this life and yet have stayed faithful.

When you want to become stronger and more physically fit, you need resistance to build muscle and strength. The same can be said of trying to grow spiritually. When things are easy, we tend to be complacent. It is in the stepping out in faith, in the challenges, and in the trials that we truly grow. It is in the praying for miracles (even more than just receiving them) that we truly see God. Remember, the point of miracles is for us to grow in our faith and for the glory to be given to our great God. The waiting is an important part of the process. The wrestling, the questioning, and the pleading softens our heart for the miracle to come.

I have known people who have prayed for God to perform a miracle in their marriage, yet their marriage ended in divorce because there must be two people open to God and trying to make a marriage work. The Bible tells us that God hates divorce[91] because he knows the hurt and pain it causes for the man, the woman, the children, and others. Yet, instead of giving up on God, I have seen people go through this difficult challenge and stay faithful to God. In the process, they have been able to see God redeem and restore. I have seen God use them to minister to others, whether by walking with others through divorce, or leading support groups and counseling people in a similar situation (and who better to help than someone who has gone through it). Other times, the hurt is redeemed through a remarriage to a godly spouse, and they end up serving the kingdom together. God specializes in redeeming and restoring. The miracle comes, but not always in the ways they expect.

The Bible is filled with examples of God at work in the midst of pain and struggle. In the gospels, we can read three different accounts of Jesus calming a storm. Most of us are either in a storm, just coming out of a storm, or about to enter one. Those passages have a lot to teach us when we feel like we are in the middle of storm and not experiencing the miracles we are hoping for.

In Mark 4, the stage is set for the miraculous calming of a storm as Jesus and his disciples stepped into a fishing boat. They pushed off into the Sea of Galilee, moving away from the crowds that Jesus had taught that day. As they rowed away from the shore, a storm picked up. This was not a little rain shower—this was a big, rough storm. The boat was thrown back and forth on huge waves and was nearly capsized.

The disciples were frantic and scared, and for experienced fishermen to be scared, this had to be a big storm. I try to picture myself in what was really just a large rowboat, in the middle of the water and far from shore, with waves tossing the boat and water coming in from all sides. The boom of the thunder. The flashes of lightning. Fighting for my life.

Maybe you have been in the middle of an awful storm like the disciples were. It seems like you are bailing water as fast as you can, but the boat continues to sink. The bills keep coming. The bad news seems to cover you. You are calling out to God, but there's no answer.

Where was Jesus in all of the commotion? You will never believe this— he was asleep. Jesus was asleep on a cushion in the front of the boat. The disciples were panic-stricken, and Jesus was not worried at all. In their fear, the disciples woke Jesus, yelling, "Teacher, don't you care if we drown?"[92]

Jesus heard their cries for help. "He got up, rebuked the wind and said to the waves, 'Quiet! Be Still!' Then the wind died down and it was completely calm. He said to his disciples, 'Why are you so afraid? Do you still have no faith?"[93] Jesus met his disciples in their worry and fear, he and reminded them to hang on to faith, even when the storm is raging.

So often, we can feel exactly like the disciples. Our lives feel out of control, and yet Jesus is perfectly calm. He is not caught off-guard with what is happening in our lives, and he is still in perfect control. As long as Jesus is in the boat, we know that a miracle is coming. Jesus was teaching his disciples (and he is teaching us) to trust him. If we call out to God, he will help calm the storms in our lives and bring us comfort and peace. We just need to trust him and have faith. In the stormy moments of our lives, we can and **must** cling to God and the basic truths that we know. Never forget that Jesus is in the boat.

Sometimes we can grow entitled. We can think that just because we are good—go to church, read our Bibles, and pray—that God somehow owes us something. Somehow we deserve for God to answer our prayers and to do miracles in our lives. The fact is, the greatest miracle of all has already happened to us. As God draws us to himself, he redeems and restores our lives. He meets us in our sin, brokenness, and depravity, and he makes us new! There is nothing we can do to earn salvation, and conversely, once we are saved in Christ, there is nothing we can do to lose our salvation.

As Ephesians 2:8-9 says, "For it is by grace you have been saved, through faith—and this not from yourselves, it is the gift of God—not by works, so that no one can boast." The greatest miracle of all has come to each of us. God has saved us by his grace and adopted us into his family. If he does nothing else for us, we have already been blessed with incredibly more than we deserve. As we learn to be grateful each day and every moment, our eyes are opened to his goodness all around us. As Paul says, "Thanks be to God for his indescribable gift!"[94] The greatest miracle has already come— God has given us the gift of his son.

IN THE DEPTHS

The points we discussed above are all important, valid, and solid truth that we can cling to. They don't change the fact that the hurt and the pain we face in this life is real and incredibly hard. We should not attempt to minimize or dismiss the pain that we and others will face. God didn't. He faced it head on. Jesus said, "I have told you these things, so that in me you may have peace. In this world you will have trouble. But take heart! I have overcome the world."[95] Jesus told us that we will have trouble in this world. This should not come as a surprise to any of us. But, Jesus also told us that he is bigger than our pain and loss. He has overcome the world!

I have found that in times of deepest loss, in the times when it is hard to see which way to go, that these truths can seem theoretical—ideas we know we should grasp but just can't. When the miracle doesn't come, it is so easy to allow these truths about God to become platitudes that bear no weight. In the depth of doubt and fear, it is easy to question everything that you know. But I urge you to hold onto God. He is still at work in your life, and he is still sovereign over all.

There is a God who created the heavens and the earth. He created everything in the universe, from a beautiful sunrise to the blossoming cherry trees, the highest mountains to the tiniest butterfly wings. This God—this mighty God—also created you, and he knows every hair on your head (which is easier for some than others). It is indeed miraculous that this great God knows you individually and intimately. He loves you, and he joins you in your pain and suffering. He is there to comfort you. 1 John 3:1 says, "See what great the love the Father has lavished on us that we should be called the children of God! And, that is what we are!" You are a child of God, and your daddy is greater than anything in this world. He is sovereign over all creation, and he loves you. As your dad, he promises to protect and provide for you. Now, that should give you all the confidence you need regardless of what life brings.

Finally, never forget the hope we have in Jesus Christ. Paul wrote, "For our light and momentary troubles are achieving for us an eternal glory that far outweighs them all."[96] When we are going through troubles, they seem anything but "light and momentary," but in the context of eternity, they are but a blip on the radar screen. Jesus came to earth and died for our sins so we can spend eternity with God. Those who are in him will join him in heaven forever. No matter what troubles this life brings, always remember that this earth is not our home. Even on our darkest nights, we can hang on to the truth that our eternity is secure.

> For I am convinced that neither death nor life, neither angels nor demons, neither the present nor the future, nor any powers, neither height nor depth, nor anything else in all creation, will be able to separate us from the love of God that is in Christ Jesus our Lord. [97]

Sometimes, in the midst of questioning God, we find that a change in perspective reveals God's presence and mercy. That friend of mine I mentioned at the start of the chapter? The one who prayed continually, asking God to do a miracle in order to heal his grandmother? Well, in the end, the cancer overcame his grandmother's physical body and she died. The miracle for which he was so desperately praying, did not come.

Or, did it?

At first, my friend was in shock. Then, after a day or so of processing, he exclaimed, "You know, my grandmother is actually healed. She loved the Lord, and while it may not look like what I wanted, she is not suffering any more, and she is healed! I know I will see her again. She is in heaven, and she is well."

This was a huge revelation for my friend, and one that has greatly impacted his life. Sometimes miracles come in simply allowing God to adjust our vision to his bigger story—teaching us to see the way he sees. Learning to view our lives under his loving hand and in light of eternity gives us an even greater view of his endless love and grace. God is always doing miracles—and the greatest ones are happening as we see ourselves growing in Christ each day.

Section 5

JUMP IN

CHAPTER 13

DIVE IN
HEART FIRST

Throughout this book, you have been reading about God's miracles and the ways he moves in the lives of people here on Earth. We have discussed what miracles look like, where to find them, and roadblocks that might prevent you from seeing miracles and getting involved in them. We have made it to the crux of this book. Now it is time to jump in.

GOD'S GREATER STORY

I believe so few people ever experience the life God has planned for them because they are content to sit on the sidelines. God invites you to be in the game. Sitting in the stands is comfortable, but you miss out on the miracles. You miss being a part of what only God can do. Through Christ, God wants to use you for his glory.

In the Old Testament, God invites Isaiah into his greater story. Isaiah takes a peek into heaven, and then he hears God say, "Whom shall I send? And who will go for us?"[98] Not even knowing the assignment, Isaiah raises his hand to say, "Here am I. Send me!" I love this! Isaiah wanted to be involved in what God was doing. He did not want to spend his life on the sidelines watching other people live their lives for God; he wanted to be in on the action. He wanted to further God's kingdom and bring glory to the Lord.

When God invites people to be a part of his greater story, most respond, "Okay, God, can you tell me exactly what you want me to do? Then I will consider it." Remember that God is not asking for our evaluation of his plans, but simply our obedience. If God told us exactly what would happen when we follow his plan, chances are that we would not believe him anyway. His plans are always bigger and richer than we could have ever dreamed for ourselves. That is why God reveals his plans throughout the journey. Like Isaiah, our call is to be ready and willing.

Many times we disqualify ourselves. We think, "God can't use me," and list off reasons. "I don't know the Bible well enough." "I am not perfect." "I've made mistakes in my past." We have all kinds of excuses. We even start to suggest other people to God. "God, what about her? She's famous; she has a lot of followers on Instagram. God, she will be better for you than I." Yet, God is calling you specifically. God will use others to accomplish his plans—you will not thwart the plans of a sovereign God—but he is giving you the opportunity to be a part of something bigger than yourself.

When God was choosing an earthly dad for his son, he called on an ordinary guy—an average Joe. Joseph was not a Pharisee or teacher of the law. Joseph did not have plenty of money to take care of Jesus and Mary with. Joseph was not influential with the Jewish leaders or Herod and the Romans. Joseph was an ordinary guy that God called to be a part of his greater story.

Joseph could have said, "No thanks, God. I have my own plans. I have a carpenter shop in Nazareth that I am thinking about franchising to other villages. I am building a house for Mary and me. I have plans for two kids, a white picket fence, and a dog." But when God spoke to Joseph, even though he did not understand, especially the "immaculate conception" thing, Joseph said yes to God. Do you think Joseph ever regretted it for a moment? No way! Joseph was a part of something way bigger than himself, and he was humbled, yet honored, to be a part of what only God can do!

AVAILABILITY OVER ABILITY

God is not as interested in our ability as he is in our availability. God is looking for willing people. He is calling you to be a part of his story; he wants you to share in the joy that comes from being a part of the work he is doing in this world; he wants you to be a part of the miracles he wants to perform. You just need to open your eyes, believe in your heart, and live for him every moment.

There are so many ways that God is calling you to take part in his story. As we talked about earlier, miracles come in all shapes and sizes. The key is to open your eyes and look around you to see where God is moving. Then find a way to use your gifts to jump in.

"What is different about you?" a college student asked my niece. "I have gone to church off and on all my life, but there is something different about you. You live it. It is who you are." My niece has seen God do miracles all her life. She is so passionate about living each day for the Lord, that joy oozes out of her. She is constantly talking to people about Jesus, praying for God to use her for his glory, and looking for opportunities to join in God's greater story. You see, we can be in church, but still not living the full Christian life. Being in church is important, but we are not called to be spectators, and my niece knows that. We are called to be in church to worship, to set our hearts on God, and to be fueled up so we are ready to be sent out and used by God.

Here is what's amazing: through the Holy Spirit, the same power that was available to Jesus for miracles is the same power available to you and me. As his disciples today, God's power is in us. Jesus said, "I tell you the truth, if you have faith as small as a mustard seed, you can say to this mountain, 'Move from here to there' and it will move. Nothing will be impossible for you."[99] The mustard seed is the smallest of all seeds. It takes just a little bit of faith and a whole lot of our great big God to see miracles actually happen.

JUST ONE STEP

The spiritual life is a journey, and we are all at different places along the way. My call to you is this: take another step in your own personal spiritual journey. Seriously, just one step—wherever you are in your spiritual journey, take a step forward in Christ.

Maybe for you it is something as simple as joining a church. Maybe you are trying to live the Christian life on your own; you want to live for God, but you have no support or encouragement. I have heard people say they are Christian, but they are not part of a church. That sounds fine, but let's think about it. Being a Christian is about responding to God's love. It is about a personal relationship with God through Jesus. God also deeply loves his church. Saying you are a Christ-follower without being a part of a church is like saying, "I am a football player, but I am not on a football team." Well, good luck with that. You will get destroyed in football if you do not have teammates to block for you or to throw the ball to. God ordained the church in part to provide support and encouragement for all of us on the journey with him. Join a local church.

Maybe a step for you is to be baptized. Baptism is an outward expression of an inward faith. Acts 2:38 says, "Repent and be baptized, every one of you, in the name of Jesus Christ for the forgiveness of your sins." Baptism follows your salvation experience. Some people say, "Well, I was baptized as an infant." That is great! However, that is more of a dedication to God. You did not make that decision. It was your parents' decision, and I am really glad they did that because they love you and wanted to raise you in a Christian home. Baptism should be your decision—your public commitment to Christ. Jesus was thirty years old when he was baptized. I have known a lot of people who cannot get past this simple step of obedience, and therefore, they stall out in their Christian life. They never progress because they are too scared or stubborn to take this simple, but life-impacting step in their spiritual journey.

Maybe a step for you is committing to spend time with the Lord each day. Maybe this has never been a consistent daily discipline for you. Prayer and reading God's word each day are the essential ingredients to a life lived for God. We live in a world of noise. There is never a quiet moment for us to even hear from God. He speaks through his still small voice, and he speaks through his word. Christianity is about a relationship with God, and a relationship involves talking and listening. There is just no substitute.

In battle, the first thing any army will try to do is cut off the opposing army's communications. They know if the enemy cannot communicate with their officers and get their orders, it will cause confusion and they will lose. Communication is essential. The same goes for us. When Satan wants to stop us from being a part of God's story, he tries to cut off our communication by giving us every excuse not to take time to pray.

Communication with God is essential. You must learn to hear from him each day. It is in this time with the Lord that you are reassured of his love for you. You find your worth and your value in Christ. You find your strength to face whatever challenges the day may bring.

We often say we are too busy to pray. Actually, I think we are too busy not to pray. We can have a lot of activity, but never really accomplish anything truly meaningful. Prayer and God's word keep us in line with his will and the story he is writing. If we make time with the Lord a priority, we will see our spiritual lives burst into action. Maybe a step for you is going on a mission trip. This idea may scare you to death. Good! That is right where God wants you. You will have to be dependent on him. On mission trips, you see God do amazing things for his glory. You meet Christ-followers in other parts of the world who are dependent on the Lord throughout each and every day. Their faith is so real and powerful. They challenge and encourage each other. They see God do miracles on a daily basis. And, when you are there, your eyes are opened to the way the rest of the world lives. You come back to your life with a renewed sense of God's presence and his calling. You go on a mission trip to help people, but what often happens in the process is that God changes you. You receive a greater glimpse of God's global story, and you want to live differently and be a part of it.

THE IMPACT OF ANOTHER "STEP"

Becky Loyd has been a member of Rolling Hills for many years. In 2007, with a bit of fear and uncertainty, Becky took a step in her spiritual journey and followed God's call on a trip to Moldova. Her life, and the lives of two young men, will never be the same. Read through this account, as written by Lisa Cannon Green:

Finding Family in a Foreign Land

Eight years ago, Becky Loyd swallowed her fear and climbed into a plane bound for Moldova. Because of that decision, she'll spend this Christmas season delivering slippers, pajamas, and hope to hundreds of abandoned children. And because of that decision, two brothers five thousand miles away have begun to call her "mom."

Tudor was twelve years old and Jony was nine when she met them in an orphanage on that first mission trip in 2007. Loyd, marketing manager of adult ministry for LifeWay Christian Resources, now talks online with them every day.

"We talk about God. We talk about money. We talk about girls sometimes," Loyd said. "I'm the closest thing they have to a mom, and they are the closest thing I have to kids. We're just figuring out how to be a family."

This month, Loyd will travel again to Moldova, a small, former Soviet Republic sandwiched between Romania and Ukraine. With the nonprofit Justice and Mercy International, she'll visit villages and orphanages, bearing gifts and sharing the story of Jesus.

"When these kids in orphanages receive a gift, it may be the first gift they've ever received," Loyd said. "They have nothing to give, but they will give you everything they have. " It changes your whole perspective on Christmas."

Staying connected

Although Moldova is a poor nation, Tudor and Jony live in an area with Internet access, and Loyd helped them buy phones.

Technology quickly transformed Loyd's newfound family, just as it has changed how she does her job. At work, social media keeps her connected with LifeWay customers. "We're doing online Bible studies with thousands of women—lots of touchpoints to engage women and churches."

And with Tudor and Jony, technology breaks down language barriers for Loyd.

"The Google Translate app has really changed my life," she said. "Sometimes it's just, 'How was school today?' But I've had some pretty intense conversations." Jony is taking English classes, so it was the best day ever when he asked, 'Will you help me with my English homework?'" "Getting a tourist visa from Moldova is a challenge," Loyd said. So far, she's been unable to bring Tudor or Jony for a visit to the United States. But she's managed to arrange a surprise trip—the brothers will fly on a plane for the first time. "It's a really cheap flight from Moldova to Vienna, so that will be their Christmas. They get to go and experience a new country."

Called to be an advocate

Loyd wasn't sure what to expect when she first reached Moldova in 2007. The poverty was unsettling, but the children touched her heart. She later recalled, "I remember knowing God had called me to be an advocate for them and not knowing how to do it"

She just kept going back. Year after year, she returned to the same orphanage—getting to know the kids, doing summer camps with them, watching them grow. Tudor and Jony became Christians. So did many others.

According to Loyd, "Now, some of those orphans have become leaders—directing music, acting as translators, and sharing the Gospel with other orphans. It's neat to see them turn around and not be ministered to, but instead pour out what the Lord has given them. I can tell an orphan their life is going to be okay and God loves them. But to hear it from somebody who has been in the same situation as they have been in is a lot more powerful."[100] This is the Christian life. Following Christ, one step at a time. Taking another step keeps you from ever becoming complacent and keeps you dialed into the heart of your father. Pretty soon, you wake up and say, "God, what do you want me to do today? How do you want to use me for your glory?" No longer will you be living in fear of what God may ask you, but living in confidence and anticipation of what he has next.

Here's the heart of the matter—discipleship is not simply about knowledge. Sometimes we mistakenly believe that being a disciple of Jesus is simply about going to another Bible study. I love Bible study; I am a pastor and I have committed my life to studying and teaching God's word. Bible study should prepare us for being involved in God's greater story, but sitting around and talking about that story is simply not enough. If the Christian life was all about Bible study, then the Pharisees would have been the most committed disciples, but the harshest words Jesus ever spoke were for the Pharisees. They knew the Old Testament better than anyone. The problem was that they did not receive Jesus nor allow God's word to move them into God's story of redemption and grace. Jesus called twelve ordinary men to follow him one step at a time. This is true discipleship. Discipleship is about transformation. The Pharisees did not move from knowledge to action. Let's not make the same mistake.

Julie and Eric felt called to help with adoption. While they do not currently feel like they are in a place to adopt themselves, they decided to use their resources to help other families who are traveling that path. When Julie heard that another family from church decided to start the process of adopting a child from Haiti, she knew she wanted to help.

There was a bit of a roadblock to helping this time. Julie and Eric were in the process of building a house, so they didn't have much wiggle room in their budget to be able to give as sizeable a gift as they wanted to. Julie thought long and hard, and she came up with a way to use another gift in order to help. Julie makes her own jam for her family, and at times she has sold some extra jars to friends in the area. She decided to make jam for the adoption fund. One hundred jars of jam later, Julie had a profit of more than five hundred dollars to donate toward the adoption.

Julie saw God moving in the lives of people through adoption. She felt called to help. She found a way to use her gifts to be part of this chapter of God's story.

Ashley is another great example of someone jumping into God's story. She is an incredible wife and mother and a great leader in her family. A few years ago, while her family lived in North Carolina, Ashley began to see a need in her own neighborhood. There were young mothers who were looking for love and guidance. Ashley saw that they not only needed support as mothers, but they also needed some spiritual mentorship. She decided to start a weekly Bible study. Other moms from her neighborhood would come to her home, enjoy coffee and breakfast, then study the Bible. When her family relocated to Tennessee, she met mothers in her new neighborhood and started another group.

Over the years, the impact of Ashley's Bible studies has been immeasurable. Her group has loved and supported women with infertility, families struggling with children who have behavioral issues, and overwhelmed young moms who just need someone in their corner. Her group has grappled with impending moves, struggled with doubt, and everything in between. God called Ashley to use her gifts of teaching and hospitality to be a part of the work he is doing in this world.

Looking around, I see people doing amazing things for Christ. I see Steve Davis, who saw a need in Moldova and urged our young church to go. That call has turned into Justice and Mercy International, which impacts literally thousands of vulnerable children around the world. I have seen community groups meet the needs of families through meals and prayers, providing immense love and comfort in both joyous and incredibly difficult times. I have seen high school students reading books and teaching preschoolers every Sunday morning as they help in Rolling Hill's children's ministry.

Friends, this does not have to be rocket science. God is moving in so many ways in and around each of us. We do not need to remain on the sidelines. We simply need to join him on the journey.

I urge you not to get bogged down by overthinking about the best use of your time or where you can make the most impact. Of course, those are noble pursuits, but they are not what God is asking of us. He asks us to offer what we have, and then he will multiply it to accomplish more for his kingdom than we could ever do on our own. We are not making changes in this world—God is. We have breath in our lungs and love in our hearts because we all still have a part to play.

Big or small, God is asking you to trust him and join in his story.

Are you willing to take the leap?

THE STRATEGY OF THE THIEF

Jesus said, "The thief comes only to steal and kill and destroy; I have come that they may have life, and have it to the full."[101] We must never forget that we have this enemy who does not want us to fulfill God's plan for our lives. God offers us a full life, yet Satan does not want us to experience it. He hates God so much that he attacks God's kids. Satan does not want us to spend time with the Lord in prayer or engage in his story. He tries to steal our joy, kill our obedience, and destroy our lives. Satan wants to keep us on the sidelines and out of the mission that God has for us.

How does Satan do this? Well, he can certainly be crafty.

One device Satan uses to keep us from fulfilling God's plan for our lives is distractions. He provides an incredible array of choices for how we can spend our time. Time with God? Time on social media? Time watching television? We have endless choices. God has blessed us with time, energy, and resources. We must periodically stop and evaluate how we are spending our time. Are we using our lives to make a difference for the glory of God? We will have to give an account of how we invest what he has entrusted to us. We must not let Satan keep us so distracted that we are robbed of the joy of being a part of God's purpose.

Satan also likes to thwart our relationship with God with unrealistic expectations. Sometimes we expect that if we are living our life for Christ, we won't have any problems. This is irrational, and we need to recognize it for the lie that it is. God is with us even in the hard times. We cannot allow Satan to steal our purpose through the unreasonable expectations that everything in life should be perfect. If we are obedient to God, regardless of the circumstances, we will see miracles unfold.

Another favorite tool Satan uses to keep us from God is comparison. When we compare ourselves to others, it can lead to envy and depression. Satan destroys our mission by telling us that we do not measure up to the people around us. We look at social media and believe that everyone is doing better than we are, forgetting that most people only post the good parts of their lives on social media, not their mess-ups. We bounce between pride and despondency when we compare ourselves to others. Comparison can kill our spiritual momentum. We have to remember that our attention should not be on others, but on God. Regardless of the circumstances we are in or we see others in, we are simply called to be faithful to God's desires for us.

Finally, Satan robs our joy through worry. We constantly play the "what if" game. "What if _____ happens?" Just fill in the blank. We lay awake at night and worry about all the negative scenarios that could pop up in our lives. Jesus said, "Who by worrying can add a single hour to your life?"[102] We need to stop wasting our time by worrying about what might happen and invest our lives for the Lord, leaving the results up to him. He is our shield and defender. He is our provider and sustainer. He will take care of us, and he will accomplish his purpose.

LIVE IT!

We experience life to the fullest by joining God in his story. But, how do we know what to do? We pray. We ask God. James writes, "If any of you lacks wisdom, he should ask God who gives generously to all without finding fault, and it will be given to you."[103] God loves it when we ask.

Asking God is the first step. He will make things clear, and then the question becomes not, "What do we do," but "Will we do what he has asked?" I believe God is constantly speaking to his disciples. So often, we know what we should do, but we are not willing to do it. Do you fit that description? Sometimes God calls us in the simple things. Recently, I was having lunch at a local restaurant with a guy from church. As we were talking, I noticed a family across the restaurant. They had two young children who were adopted from another culture. There was also another young adult with them. I had never seen them before, but for whatever reason, God spoke, not with a loud, audible voice, but so clearly that it was just as obvious. "Buy their meal." There I was, engaged in a conversation with this guy about what God was doing at church, and at the exact same time, God was telling me to buy a random family's meal. My first thought was, "Are you sure?" Again, the voice. "Buy their meal." Then I began to wonder about that family's story. Were they Christians? Was it best to do this? Again, the voice. "Buy their meal." I began to worry about how much they were ordering, and if their tab was going to be really expensive. (I know, that was not a super spiritual response.) Again, the voice said, "Buy their meal."

After a while, it became a matter of obedience. It did not matter what they would do with the blessing, or even how much it cost. It was pure and simple obedience. I gave the waiter my credit card and told him what I wanted to do. Then I left. They had no idea it was me, and I won't ever know what they thought. But that did not matter. It was not about me, but about God. He wanted to buy their meal that day, and he just happened to allow me to be a part of that plan.

As you pray, God will make things clear to you. God is not a God of confusion, but a God of clarity. He wants you to know his will and to fulfill his calling in your life. Through his Holy Spirit, God will prompt your heart. He will lead you. Whether it is buying a meal for someone or starting a church—small or big—God will invite you to join in his story.

The incredible news is that God is not finished with any of us yet. He is still at work, conforming us to the image of his son,[104] and using us as his hands and feet to share his love with a world in need. Will you join God in what he is doing? Will you put aside your plans and follow Christ? Take a step and watch God do what only he can do. Trust that God can and will accomplish his plans. There is joy in the journey. Step out and join him.

CHAPTER 14

LEAP INTO
YOUR LEGACY

You and I get one shot at this life—one opportunity. This is our time, so let's make the most of it. Let's achieve our God-given potential and truly invest our lives for his glory.

So what now? How do we live in a way that reflects our love for our Savior and allows us to be a part of God's movements in this world? I hope this chapter gives you some ideas on how to join in.

IT ALL STARTS WITH LOVE

As you pray and ask God to guide you to live according to his agenda, you will find yourself truly come alive. You will be more connected to God and fall more in love with him. Jesus told us that the two greatest commandments are to love God and love our neighbor.[105] Each day is successful if you are able to grow in your love of God and for others. How do you love God more? Spend time with him. Through prayer, you will not only be guided by God to what he wants you to do, but you will come to know God himself. You will know what he loves and what he does not. You will understand his character and his heart. You will desire more and more to be in his presence. This is the beautiful truth of Christianity—it is a love relationship with your creator through his Jesus, his son.

Teach me your way, O Lord, that I may rely on your faithfulness; give me an undivided heart, that I may fear your name. I will praise you, O Lord my God, with all my heart; I will glorify your name forever. For great is your love toward me; you have delivered me from the depths, from the realm of the dead.[106]

As you fall more in love with God, you will understand more of the depth of his love for you. You will feel his grace and be compelled forward in your spiritual journey. As you take the next step, your faith and trust in him will grow. It is a beautiful relationship—the one you were created to experience. As you grow in your love for God, you cannot help but love others as well.

Loving others is incredibly important. Love is compelling. The opposite of love is not hate; it is apathy. You can't be complacent and love. If you love, you will care. If you love God, you will care about what he cares about. You will be compelled to get involved in this world and to make a difference. As you grow in your love for God, you will experience a transformation in your own heart. Your own personal desires will subside and God's desires will move you to love others.

YOUR UNIQUE GIFTS

God has wired you to make a difference in this world. There is no one in the world exactly like you. No one has your same gifts, resources, or sphere of influence. God has a unique plan for your life: to draw you to himself, to fill you with his Spirit, and to use you for his glory.

It's easy to look at social media posts and want to do exactly what we see someone else doing. But I urge you, do not try to be someone else. As we discussed earlier, comparison is one of Satan's favorite tactics to keep you from taking part in God's work in this world. You will never experience your amazing role in God's story by trying to live someone else's life. As you pray, you will begin to understand more of what God is uniquely calling you to do. You just have to do it.

So many times I have heard the question, "What if I get it wrong?" People want to know what happens if what we choose to do is not what God had in mind. Rest easy. What God wants is for you to do something to love others. If you are in conversation with him, you cannot pick anything wrong. You can't mess up! You can trust that God knows your gifts and will guide you to the best way to use them.

BE INTENTIONAL

As we discussed in our last chapter, God will bring opportunities for you to join in his work by speaking to your mind as you pray. Whether it is cooking someone a meal or going on a mission trip, God will show you situations where you can step in and demonstrate his love. In addition to responding to the Spirit's leading, there is also a responsibility for every Christ-follower to be proactive in understanding God's specific call for his or her life.

God wants us to be intentional about our time in prayer. Not only are we called to pray in the mornings or at night, but we are called to pray throughout our day. We can take moments during the day to share our joys and gratitude with him. God wants us to develop an intimate relationship with him in which we are constantly aware of and listening to him. As God speaks, we respond. We serve. We love. We step in and help people in his name.

God also wants us to be intentional with our lives. We should not be simply wandering aimlessly and helping people only when we happen to come across them. There is a very clear direction for our lives. God wants us to be intentional with our decisions and commitments. We have limited amounts of time and money. Therefore, we must invest these well for the maximum impact for his kingdom. As we begin to understand how God has wired us and what he wants to accomplish through us, we can truly live the immeasurably more life.

For example, if God has wired you to be a teacher, then you need to be the best teacher you can be. You need to impact the next generation for his glory. That is how he wired you, and that is what will bring the most fulfillment in your life. Focus on the students God has entrusted to you. There will be opportunities along the way to help address specific needs or even go on mission trips where you can use your gifts to help children and students in other parts of your community or the world. These are not interruptions, but should instead be seen as divine appointments. Even so, there is a specific path on which God has placed you. As a teacher, you are on the way to fulfilling your God-given potential, and in that role, you will have a great impact on the kingdom as you disciple others.

Maybe God has wired you to make money. You are successful at whatever you undertake in the business world. You have favor with investors, vendors, and other business leaders. God will use you to help others. He may call you to fund groups that help the poor, the orphaned, or the widowed. If so, give to groups that call to your heart. Set goals for yourself, not just about the amount of money you can make, but about the amount of money you can give. Again, there will be divine appointments along the way to share Christ with coworkers, serve in leadership at church, and more. Through it all, be intentional with what God has called you to do. Leverage your gifts and your sphere of influence for his purposes.

Be intentional. When you find your sweet spot in life, that is where you will reach your maximum potential. That is where you will experience the immeasurably more life. There will be amazing ministry opportunities along the way, but keep pressing into God's ultimate plan for you.

FIND YOUR GIFTS AND PASSIONS

As you walk in this love relationship with God, he will give you clarity about your gifts and passions. Each of us was created for a purpose in this place and at this time. Ask God to reveal the unique ways he has gifted you. Do you love children? Are you excellent at organizing large events? Do you thrive in finance and accounting? Do you love to communicate through writing, photography, or music? Each of these gifts can help you play an important part in God's story. At the same time, pray for God to call attention to the passions he placed in you. Does your heart break for the poor and hungry? Do you feel called to help orphans near you or in other parts of the world? Do you see a need for ministry in your own neighborhood? Ask God to guide you to a specific place that you can serve according to your passions.

Through prayer, we can ask God to open our eyes to the needs around us. Ask God to reveal to you where your passions and the needs of the world intersect. Ask him to open your ears to hear pain, worry, and loneliness. Think about how God wired you to impact the world. How can you leverage your gifts and resources?

As we pray, we intentionally seek to be a part of his story. Martin Luther King, Jr., once said, "Prayer is a marvelous and necessary supplement to our feeble efforts, but it is a dangerous substitute."[107] He hit the nail right on the head. Prayer is absolutely essential to our efforts in doing God's work in this world, but we must not hesitate to act.

There may not be a lightning-bolt moment of clarity as to the role God wants you to play. As we talked about earlier, God reveals his story in his timing. We have to step out in faith, trusting God to reveal his plan to us as we go. Most of our steps will be small steps of obedience as we meet the next need that God places in front of us—beginning with the understanding that our gifts and passions will impact every area of our lives. You might need to simplify your schedule and prioritize activities that feed your heart and soul. It might mean you need to forgive yourself for your past. It might mean you need to finally make a budget plan—and stick to it—so you can use the material gifts God has given you to help others.

Finally, it is incredibly important to recognize that jumping into God's story is going to change your life. This is a great thing, but I urge you not to become impatient or get overwhelmed. Life change does not happen overnight. Sustainable life change is a gradual process that God is ready to lead you through.

START SIMPLY, BUT SIMPLY START

When the time comes to jump in, the possibilities of ways to get involved in God's story are endless. Some people find the variety of possibilities freeing, while others find the number of opportunities frustrating. In order to help those of you who may be a bit overwhelmed at the possibilities laid out before you, let's look at some places you might begin.

Start in your home.

Sometimes, it can be easy to overlook the very significant roles God has placed you in within your own home and family. As a believer in Jesus Christ, you can be a light to the world, and oftentimes that world starts right in your own house. How is God calling you to lead your family? What role is God calling you to play in the life of your roommate or your extended family?

Parents, a special note for you: there is a very real role you need to play in raising up children who love God and who want to live life for him. Your obedience day in and day out—joyfully doing the work of your home, setting an example of time with the Lord, teaching your children about Jesus and his love for us—is vital kingdom work. Please do not buy into the lie that success needs to come from outside of the home. You have no more important call than the role you are placed in as a parent.

Ideas on where start at home:

- Model a Christian walk for others. Spend time in the word. Spend time in prayer. Speak out loud about your love for the Lord and your gratitude for his grace and mercy.
- Simplify your life. How can you bless others with your blessings? Give clothes to local organizations that help those in need, such as homeless shelters or refugee organizations.
- Speak truth to your children. Teach them about the greatness of our God. Follow the commands of Deuteronomy 6: Teach your child at home and on the road, at the beginning and end of the day.[108] Make conversation about Christ part of your daily life. If your kids know more about football or Disney movies than God, you are missing the boat.

Connect with your community.

God has built you for community, and he has placed you where you are for a reason. Who are the people around you—your neighbors, your coworkers, and others—who you see every day? Make an effort to connect with them and take an interest in their lives. Pray for them. Through conversation and prayer, you may find ways to meet needs in their lives in very tangible ways. God calls all of us to love our neighbors, and connecting with them is the first step.

Ideas on where to start in your community:

- Invite someone to coffee or lunch, and connect over conversation.
- Shovel snow or mow lawns for your neighbors.
- Provide meals for someone who is sick or hurting.
- Write an encouraging note to a friend or coworker.
- Call a mom you know and offer a free night of babysitting.
- Start a Bible study at work, at school, or in your neighborhood.
- Teach Sunday school or lead a small group at church.
- Visit people in the hospital and pray with them.

Partner with an organization doing good work in your local area.

You do not have to travel around the world to see great need. In each of our communities, there are groups serving the least of these, the people Jesus calls us to care for and love. Seek them out. How can you come alongside these groups and help their efforts? Check out the groups that you feel are doing some of the best work in your area, and see where you can join them.

Ideas on where to start with local organizations:

- Donate food or time to your local food bank. You could even organize a food drive.
- Support the work of foster parents or become one yourself.

- Donate clothes or home goods to a refugee organization that welcomes people to your area or to a thrift store that supports local work. Collect donated items from your neighbors as well.
- Help at-risk students with homework. Involve your family in this effort.
- Seek ways that you can support these organizations as a volunteer or donor.

Set your sights on the needs of people around the world.

Does your heart break for the plight of people around the world? Do you feel called to help share the Gospel with people who have been previously unreached? There are a number of incredible organizations already doing amazing work in every nation of the world. Jump in and be a part of what God is doing.

Ideas on where to start with global missions:

- Go on a mission trip.
- Sponsor a child through an organization like Justice and Mercy International.
- Donate time and money to organizations that you believe in.
- Support and pray for missionaries around the world.

Most importantly, **start doing something**. There may be several ideas on this list that sound good to you, and you may have several more of your own. Or you may still feel unsure about where God is calling you. In either case, I urge you to remember that while you cannot do everything, you can do something. Pray for God's guidance and support as you step forward in faith to take part in his work. I promise that the feeling of being a part of his story is one of the most incredible things you will ever experience—do not let fear hold you back from an immeasurably more life.

BE FAITHFUL

As you step out, you have to keep in mind that an immeasurably more life is not just about how you start. The aim is not just to do good things. It is more than that. The overall goal of that life is faithfulness to God—holding on to Christ and growing deeper in faith throughout your life. In the New Testament, the book of Hebrews outlines what is known as the "Faith Hall of Fame."[109] It is amazing to read the different people listed: Abraham, Moses, David, and more. Not one person in this list was perfect. They all made mistakes, but they were all intentional about walking with God through their entire lives. They never quit. Despite the challenges and difficulties, they held on to God.

Solomon is the Biblical figure who is most disappointing to me. This guy was the son of David, the greatest king of Israel. He had a great father, a wonderful family, and lots of material blessings. He had a great start. He grew up knowing about God, had an amazing heritage, and had some incredible leadership opportunities. He discovered his gifts and passions, and God blessed him. He was the wisest and wealthiest man who ever lived. He built the Temple to God and blessed it. Solomon was on a roll.

Over time, Solomon started to drift away from God. He fell in love with women—a lot of them. He had 700 wives and 300 concubines![110] That was definitely not a part of God's plan. God's plan was always one man and one woman, but Solomon became distracted. He fell in love with the things of the world, and he stopped being the godly king that the Lord had designed him to be. At the end of his life, the kingdom was split in two because of Solomon's disobedience.

Like Solomon, it can be easy for us to drift away from the Lord. We never just slip into a deeper relationship with God. We have to be intentional about building intimacy with him. The goal of our lives is faithfulness to God, not being perfect or achieving some great success. God can and will redeem and restore our lives. God will bring the victories. We are called to simply hang on to God all of our days. The Bible tells us:

Therefore, since we are surrounded by such a great cloud of witnesses, let us throw off everything that hinders and the sin that so easily entangles. And let us run with perseverance the race marked out for us, fixing our eyes on Jesus, the pioneer and perfecter of our faith. For the joy set before him endured the cross, scorning its shame, and sat down at the right hand of the throne of God. Consider him who endured such opposition from sinners, so that you will not grow weary and lose heart.[111]

Think about this: there are people who have gone before us who have lived this life well. They lived the lives laid out for them, and now they are in heaven cheering us on. These are not only the people we read about in the Bible like Abraham, Moses, and David, but also many others like grandparents, great-grandparents, or even close friends and influential teachers—people who lived their lives for Christ. Think about the people who have invested in you. They are cheering for you to make the most of your life.

We each have a calling and a responsibility to run the course that God has marked for us. God has a unique plan for our lives. We are on a lifetime journey with him, so let's run this race well. Let's not grow weary and lose heart. Our call is to faithfulness. We accomplish this by setting our eyes on Jesus—not getting distracted with the things of this world like Solomon, who was consumed with money and the opposite sex—and being intentional with our lives.

Are you faithful? Are you growing in your love relationship with God? Are you more in love with God today than when you first accepted Christ as your personal Lord and Savior? Are you growing in your love for God and your love for others? Are you serving him passionately?

FINISH WELL

At the end of his life Paul writes, "I have fought the good fight, I have finished the race, I have kept the faith. Now there is in store for me the crown of righteousness which the Lord, the righteous judge, will award me on that day—and not only me, but also to all those who have longed for his appearing."[112] This is my prayer for you and me. I pray you and I finish well. I pray that we experience the immeasurably more life here in this world and then share eternity together with our Lord. I pray that we fulfill God's desire for us in this life knowing our eternity is secure forever.

Wherever you are today, just know that the rest of your life can be lived as part of God's amazing story. God has placed his hand upon you and his Holy Spirit in you. Start right now. Make a commitment to Christ to live each day for him, to remain faithful, and to finish well. Don't quit now! God has a great plan for you, and the immeasurably more life awaits!

CHAPTER 15

YOU ARE
NEVER ALONE

"Jeff, I'm a miracle," Michael said when I walked in the door. "This new doctor just came in and looked at all my scans. He said, 'There is no way you should be alive. People do not survive this kind of head injury.'" A year earlier, Michael, who was in his mid-forties, had sustained a traumatic brain injury. Yet here he was, alive and well. As a husband and father, Michael has come to see this as a wakeup call from God. "My life was out of control, and God used this to bring me back to him." Michael went to church before his accident, but he had been living for himself. His lifestyle and habits looked more like the rest of world's than Christ's. Today, he is thriving as an amazing husband and father and investing passionately in God's church and his kingdom. He is embracing every moment. Michael is a miracle.

As we have seen throughout this book, God is constantly doing miracles. He is at work in the lives of people all around us. He is redeeming, restoring, and making all things new. Opening our eyes to God's miracles is how we take part in God's story.

Now, here's the incredible promise of that immeasurably more life: it means you are never alone! God is with you. The creator of the universe, the sustainer of life, the giver of hope is with you, and he is for you. How awesome! Whatever you are facing today, realize that you are not alone. So many times we feel like everything is crashing down on us. We feel isolated and trapped. Into a world of insecurity, hate, and desperation enters the God of love and grace, the God who promises to "never leave you nor forsake you."[113]

Jesus concluded his physical time on earth by bringing his disciples together on the Mount of Olives. Jesus lived thirty-three sinless years, performed many amazing miracles, and conquered our greatest enemy—death. His disciples had been with Jesus for three years. Just before he ascended into heaven, he looked them in the eyes and gave them what we know as the Great Commission: "Therefore go and make disciples of all nations, baptizing them in the name of the Father, and of the Son and of the Holy Spirit, and teaching them to obey everything I have commanded you."[114] Jesus commissioned his disciples to share his story with others.

This commission had to be a little intimidating for the disciples. They had seen Jesus do miracles, and now he was passing the torch to them. They had to be frightened and uncertain about what was to come, but then Jesus gave them this amazing promise: "And surely I am with you always, to the end of the age."[115] Wow! As he sent his disciples into the world, Jesus promised that they would never be alone; he would always be with them.

That same promise extends to you and me as well. How incredible! You are never alone. Regardless of what comes your way in life, Christ Jesus is always with you. In addition, he invites you to lock arms with other believers as you go forward in the journey. The disciples had Christ's presence and they had each other, and believers today can rest in that same promise. This is the importance of church and community. As a Christ-follower, you are never alone.

SHADRACH, MESHACH, AND ABEDNEGO

One of my favorite stories in the Bible is about three guys who totally lived their lives for God. Their faith in God and dedication to him is inspiring, and their story provides a lot of points of comfort and guidance for believers today.

These three guys were sharp. They loved the Lord, and they had big plans. But, their country, Judah, was conquered by another nation, and these three young men were all deported into exile by the Babylonians, the conquering nation. However, through it all, God was with them. Maybe your life feels a bit like you are living in a foreign land. Remember that God is with you.

Because they were smart, strong, and had leadership potential, the three young men were quickly drafted into the king of Babylon's service. They had to take on jobs they did not want. This was not the plan they had for their lives, but God was still at work. Maybe you find yourself in a job you don't like. Trust that God is with you. Focus on your relationship with him and do a good job where you are. These guys stayed faithful to God, and they did a good job. In fact, they were so good that they were promoted to oversee different affairs in the province of Babylon.

One day, the king, their boss, made a really bad decision. He built a huge statue and wanted everyone to worship it, and the people did what the king asked, except for those three guys. They knew it was not right to worship anything or anyone but God. The king found out, and he was furious. He brought the three men before him, and he told them that if they did not bow down and worship this statue, they would be killed. Today, if we stand up for what is right in the workplace, the worst thing that can happen is that we lose our jobs. For these guys, it was a matter of life and death.

So, there they were—standing before the king who was telling them to do something they did not agree with, something that went against what God said. Here's how they responded: "We do not need to defend ourselves before you in this matter. If we are thrown into the blazing furnace, the God we serve is able to deliver us from it, and he will deliver us from Your Majesty's hand. But even if he does not, we want you to know, Your Majesty, that we will not serve your gods or worship the image of gold you have set up."[116] Wow! That response was bold and demonstrated great confidence in God.

Their response made the king even more furious. He ordered the furnace to be heated up seven times hotter than normal. Then he had these three guys bound and thrown into the fire. The furnace was so hot that the guards who threw them in were engulfed in the flames.

As the king watched, a miracle unfolded. Listen to this: "Then King Nebuchadnezzar leaped to his feet in amazement and asked his advisers, 'Weren't there three men that we tied up and threw into the fire?' They replied, 'Certainly, Your Majesty.' He said, 'Look! I see four men walking around in the fire, unbound and unharmed, and the fourth looks like a son of the gods.'"[117] Yes! Jesus was with these three guys in the fire. "Nebuchadnezzar then approached the opening of the blazing furnace and shouted, 'Shadrach, Meshach and Abednego, servants of the Most High God, come out! Come here!'"[118]

The pre-incarnate Jesus came and walked with these guys in the fire. This same Jesus is with you. He has promised to "never leave you nor forsake you."[119] He is with you in a foreign land. He is with you in a tough job situation. He is with you in relational uncertainty. He is with you, and because he is with you, a miracle could be just around the corner. God is always working with you and for you.

MOVE FORWARD WITH CONFIDENCE

God's miracles did not just happen in the accounts in the Bible. Miracles happen today. They are for all followers of Christ—ordinary people like you and me—who are passionately pursuing God. Why? Because Jesus is with us. In essence, miracles are Christ working through us for his glory in a needy world.

God is always faithful to his promises. That is his character. You can look at a rainbow and remember God's promise to Noah. You can go back to Abraham and see generations of his promise. You can even trek with the children of Israel and see the lengths God goes to keep his promise. Once you are in a covenant relationship with God, you are never alone! Listen to this promise to Israel, his people, in the Old Testament book of Isaiah:

But now, this is what the Lord says—he who created you, Jacob, he who formed you, Israel: "Do not fear, for I have redeemed you. I have summoned you by name; you are mine. When you pass through the waters, I will be with you; and when you pass through the rivers, they will not sweep over you. When you walk through the fire, you will not be burned; the flames will not set you ablaze. For I am the Lord your God, the Holy One of Israel, your Savior."[120]

By God's grace, we are his people and part of his covenant through Christ. God has been faithful to his people, Israel, and now, through Christ, God is faithful to us. How awesome that in our sin and total depravity, God came to us! As you read the birth narrative of Jesus, here is what God tells us: "The virgin will conceive and give birth to a son, and they will call him Immanuel (which means "God with us")."[121] God wrapped himself in flesh, and he came to us. This is what makes Christianity different from every other major world religion. Other religions center on man trying to get to God: if I can do enough good things, then maybe God will accept me. If my good outweighs my bad, then maybe God will elevate me to a higher state. Conversely, Christianity is God coming to man. In the midst of our hurt, pain, and brokenness, God comes to us. In the midst of our sin, depravity, and mess, God comes near. We can never be completely perfect on our own, so God sends his son, Jesus, to us.

Jesus was born into a world of hate. The Jews hated the Romans, and the Romans hated the Jews; the Jews hated the Samaritans, and the Samaritans hated the Jews, and the list goes on. Yet, Jesus came in the midst of all that hate with a new message—a message of love. Love. Jesus loves us so much that he left the throne room of heaven and came down to earth. God is here, and he is with you.

What, then, shall we say in response to these things? If God is for us, who can be against us? He who did not spare his own Son, but gave him up for us all—how will he not also, along with him, graciously give us all things? Who will bring any charge against those whom God has chosen? It is God who justifies. Who then is the one who condemns? No one. Christ Jesus who died—more than that, who was raised to life—is at the right hand of God and is also interceding for us. Who shall separate us from the love of Christ? Shall trouble or hardship or persecution or famine or nakedness or danger or sword? As it is written: "For your sake we face death all day long; we are considered as sheep to be slaughtered." No, in all these things we are more than conquerors through him who loved us.[122] How amazing this is! God is greater than anything we face, and he promises to always be with us. Nothing in this world is too great for him to handle. Sometimes we may think, "But what if I mess up? What if I do something so bad, and then God leaves me?" As you can see, there is nothing you can do to lose your eternal security in God through Christ. Think about it. If you did not do anything to earn it, then what can you do to lose it? God is always there for you! This means that we can be incredibly confident in God. He is always faithful, and he calls us to faithfulness as well—to be faithful to him, to his calling in our lives, and to our brothers and sisters in Christ. As we are faithful, we see miracles. As we see miracles, we are led into a deeper relationship with God and into a greater love for his people.

In the Old Testament, God's people were only the Israelites, but through Christ, today the church becomes God's people. As 1 Peter 2:9 says, "But you are a chosen people, a royal priesthood, a holy nation, God's special possession, that you may declare the praises of him who called you out of darkness and into his wonderful light." All along the way, God has brought people to the church who have different gifts, talents, and abilities. As God is working in one person's life, others grow confident of his presence with us. This is why it is so important to be a part of a local church, a local body of Christ-followers who share the same joy and passion for his name.

GOING FORWARD WITH BOLDNESS

Because we have God with us, we have the confidence to live each day for his glory. This assurance calls us to be bold. Our confidence in God's love should never lead us to complacency, or take us away from people or from a hurting world. Rather it should give us the boldness to actively engage in the world and share God's love with others.

As the first disciples to Jesus stood on the Mount of Olives looking up as Jesus ascended into heaven, they did not know what to do. They had heard the commission Jesus gave them to go forward and make disciples, and they trusted that Jesus would always be with them, but they stood there bewildered and confused. They probably thought, "Yes, God is with us, but how in the world are we going to be able to accomplish what he laid out for us to do?"

How many times have we thought this same thing? We go to church or to a Bible study and we walk away wondering, Am I ready to do this? Am I ready to take the Gospel to the nations? Am I ready to disciple my kids? Am I ready to tell someone at school or at work about Christ? Although we have the assurance that God is with us, we still need the boldness to engage in his calling.

For most of us, it is not about knowing what to do. It is really about simply being bold enough to act and engage in God's call. The disciples spent three years with Jesus. After the ascension, they knew what to do; they just needed to go live it. They could have gone home, kicked back, and said to themselves, "That was an amazing three years. Most people will never have that kind of experience. Lucky me." If they had done that, they would have missed the miracles that were still to come. They would have missed out on God's will for their lives, and they would have missed out on having an incredible impact on the world that we still see today. Some of the best times of their lives and ministries were still to come.

The account of Jesus's ascension does not end when he leaves. We read about the disciples: "They were looking intently up into the sky as he was going, when suddenly two men dressed in white stood beside them."[123] It must have been pretty funny as these eleven guys were looking up into the sky and the angels showed up, stood beside them, and looked up with them. "'Men of Galilee,' they said, 'why do you stand here looking into the sky? This same Jesus, who has been taken from you into heaven, will come back in the same way you have seen him go into heaven.'"[124] That was all the prompting the disciples needed—it was go time, not the time to stand around and look up into heaven. It was time to go live their lives for Christ and his glory. They got it, and they lived it! The book of Acts is all about the acts of the disciples boldly living their lives for Jesus. Their numbers quickly grew into the thousands. They witnessed great miracles, but also endured challenges along the way. Through it all, they remained faithful, committed, and bold.

To me, the real miracle in the book of Acts is the transformation of these disciples. Jesus called ordinary fisherman to follow him, and they only spent three years following Jesus. Many of us have spent a lot more time than that following Christ. When Jesus was arrested, they all scattered. When Jesus was crucified, they were all afraid. When Jesus was resurrected, they were all confused. Yet, when the Holy Spirit came, they were all transformed. Discipleship is about transformation. Jesus took those eleven men and changed the world. They went from sitting on the sidelines, scared that they too would be arrested, to boldly leading a movement of Christ that has changed our world.

The world today is looking for bold disciples—not people who are perfect, but people who are so filled with the Holy Spirit that they are willing to push past the fear and uncertainty in order to run to the front lines of ministry. Whether opening your home to a refugee family, adopting an orphan, engaging in a spiritual conversation with someone at work, or going to live in another country on mission, the call is to be bold for Christ and his kingdom. The people who have really embraced living for Christ are the people who have stepped out and seized the opportunities God sets before them.

As God's Holy Spirit comes into your life, he transforms you, and as you respond to God's love in your life, the strength of the Holy Spirit grows. You are no longer alone—God is with you. You are no longer afraid—God is for you. You are no longer the same—God is in you. Now, there may be moments when you feel alone, afraid, or hesitant, but overall you are different. You are changed. You must own your new nature! You do not want to live as a caterpillar when you are butterfly. You want to fly! You want to live each day with the boldness and assurance of God's love.

When we started Rolling Hills, we met Tom. Tom was in his twenties and had been living in another state. Knowing it was time for a change, he had moved to Tennessee, leaving the security of everything he knew to come to a place where he knew very few people. He was one of the first fifteen people at our church, and God has done immeasurably more in his life.

That first night in the apartment clubhouse, Tom met a girl on our team. They fell in love, and within a year, were married. He began growing in his relationship with God each day and began to understand his calling to be the spiritual leader of his home. Tom and his wife served at church every week. Soon, he felt God leading him to start a business. He made a commitment to God to always be growing in his giving and to tithe, not just personally, but also on the business.

He and his wife had a child, and then their second child was born with Downs Syndrome. They immediately got involved in Best Buddies. Tom realized his need to be present for his family—spiritually, emotionally and physically—so he began working out and lost about sixty pounds. The family bought a new home and immediately opened it to a small group every Monday night for new people to study the word of God and grow in their faith. Then he developed a passion for helping refugees in the Middle East and started to go on mission trips to serve there. Looking at his life today, he is a miracle. Just like the early disciples, God transformed his life.

Whether an orphan in Moldova, a stay-at-home mom in the United States, or a child in the Amazon, there is something incredible that happens as Jesus changes a heart and a life. Transformation doesn't mean everything in life is easy and there are no challenges to face, but it does mean that God is present. Living life with this confidence changes everything.

Here's what it all comes down to: **you are the miracle!** Stop for a minute and reflect on your life. Think about all that God has done—the breath in your lungs, the joy in your heart, the roof over your head, the food on your table, the goodness of God in your life each day. Think about where you were before you met Christ and how God has redeemed and restored you. You are being transformed, not because of anything you have done, but through the work of God. He brought you into this world for a reason and a purpose. He loves you and he has been pursuing you all of your life. The God of the universe is with you, and when you live each day with him, there is nothing greater! This is how you were created to live.

This is the immeasurably more life!

CONCLUSION

ALL GLORY
TO GOD

Do you feel that hunger for more in your life? As you have read, there is definitely a God who longs for you to experience more—immeasurably more. As you embrace the life he has called you to live, you will fall more in love with him, and your eyes will be opened to his work in this world. God is inviting you to experience all that he has for you.

Are you ready to take the leap? All you have to do is ask. Every morning for the rest of your life, wake up and pray, "God, I want to know you, and I want to live my life for you today. Open my eyes to what you are doing. Allow me to embrace the life that you have for me. God, I am yours. All for you and for your glory!"

When you pray this prayer, get ready! God will answer. God will open your eyes and your life will come alive. You will begin to see God do miracles. You will see God do things in you and through you that you would never have dreamed. You will see life transformation all around you, and this will give you a hunger for even more—more of God and a desire to invest more in his greater story.

It does not matter what your job is, how much money you make, if you are married or single—your life circumstances do not dictate your ability to be a part of what God is doing in this world. What does matter is that you are pressing deeper into the heart of God and being obedient to do his will. What matters is that you are living life to the full and experiencing all God has for you. What matters is that you accomplish what God has for you in your life.

I know hundreds of people who are investing their lives in God's call and truly experiencing this immeasurably more life. Some you have read about here, but there are countless others. They are not perfect, but they are hungry for more of God and his transforming power. These are ordinary people who are living out the call of Christ in their lives—people in the United States and around the globe who have chosen to live not simply for the money, power, and success this world has to offer, but to live differently. These people are experiencing joy—a depth and richness to their lives. God is transforming them and using them for his glory in the lives of others.

As we try to discern where we can join God in his work in this world, it is important that we stay in close relationship with him. We all want to know God's will for our lives, and he tells us. In 1 Thessalonians, Paul writes that as followers of Jesus we should, "Rejoice always, pray continually, give thanks in all circumstances; for this is God's will for you in Christ Jesus."[125] What does that mean for us?

- **Be joyful always.** Now that you are opening your eyes to God's work in this world, what do you see? Rejoice in what God is doing, and rejoice in his saving grace for you. Concentrate on all the ways that God has taken care of you—the way he has provided for you with salvation, food, shelter, family, friends, church, and more. Thanking him for his goodness and grace in your life gives you confidence as you go forward. Focusing on all God has done for you causes you to live your life with joy.

- **Pray continually.** Because we do not physically see God in front of us, it is easy for us to make our prayers to him just a task on our daily checklist. But our relationship with God can and should be more than that! God is our heavenly father and our friend. How do you communicate with your best friend here on earth? When you receive good news or bad news, do you call or text? Do you celebrate the joys of life and band together in the struggles? This is what God wants you to do with him. As you go through your day, spend time talking with God, asking for help, rejoicing in his glory, praying for yourself and others. Praying continually becomes a daily conversation with the giver and sustainer of life. His presence should bring you comfort and strength each moment of your day.

- **Give thanks in all circumstances.** No matter what circumstances you find yourself in throughout your life, the true nature of God will never change. He loves you. He guides your steps. He hears your prayers. He also reveals new mercies and miracles every day. As you open your eyes to his work in this world, you should join with other believers in prayerful thanksgiving. Whatever comes your way—the good and the bad—you can be thankful. Romans 8:28 says, "And we know that in all things God works for the good of those who love him, who have been called according to his purpose." This doesn't say "all things are good," because some are not. This is a fallen, broken world. It does say that God is always working—redeeming, restoring and making things right.

As we come to the end of this book, I want you to know that you have the power to see what God is doing in this world, and he is inviting you to join in his story. You have the opportunity to open your eyes and to be a part of the miracles that God wants to do in you as well as through you for his glory! Will there be difficulties? Yes! We have talked about roadblocks that can stymie us as we pursue the incredible life God has for us. Our past can tell us lies, we can be afraid of what others think, and we have an enemy who does not want us to succeed. We also need to be aware of how the world will try to rationalize the supernatural.

People in western culture today try to explain miracles away. Christians debate whether the Israelites crossed the Red Sea or the Reed Sea. People credit modern day medicine with healing people without recognizing the healing touch of God. (Can God heal through medicine? Of course! Where did the miracle to develop the medicine come from in the first place? We pray for miracles and healings, and many times God answers with medical breakthroughs.) God and science are not mutually exclusive. Some of the greatest thinkers of all time have been Christ-followers. It is God who created this planet and who is continually at work redeeming and restoring. Deep down, we all know that there is more than we can see.

Why do miracles continue to happen today in a society that seems so bent on disbelief? Miracles happen so God receives glory. Miracles point us to God and remind us that no matter what we face in life, our God is greater! Miracles happen every day.

I love that for his first miracle Jesus performed, he turned water to wine. Jesus took the ordinary (water) and made it extraordinary (wine). This type of miracle is God's specialty. If you read about the event recorded in John 2, you will see that the water turned to wine was the best wine at the party! This reflects the heart of God and his desire for each of us. God takes ordinary people like you and me, and through his grace, we become extraordinary. God wants us to experience the best, and to be all that he desires.

Miracles are not reserved only for pastors, priests, and other "holy" people. **Miracles are for all followers of Christ**—common, every day, ordinary people, just like you and me. People who simply place their lives in the hands of the master are the ones who see the miracles, and as we see God moving in the world, he receives our praise.

As you discover ways be a part of God's story and as you witness his miracles in this world, I pray that you also find ways to share the joy of this immeasurably more life with others. I pray that you can help others open their spiritual eyes to the presence of God in their lives. I pray that God will work through you to share his message of hope and love with those around you. I pray that your story can be part of God transforming the ordinary into the extraordinary by leading people to himself.

Our God has done immeasurably more in each of our lives. Just like the children of Israel, we were in bondage. We were slaves to sin with no hope and no help. The children of Israel called out to God for a deliverer, and he sent Moses. When we called out to God for help, he sent his own son, Jesus Christ. When we were dead in our sins and transgressions, he made us alive in Christ. Here's the incredible part: when all we asked for was salvation—freedom from sin—what we received was so much more. "See what great love the Father has lavished on us, that we should be called children of God! And that is what we are!"[126] God not only gave us freedom, but he invited us to be a part of his family—heirs with Christ to the family fortune and to eternal life with him.

This is the greatest miracle of all! Remember, if God does not do another miracle in your life, then you have more than enough through Christ. You are free from sin and death, and you are forever his. God is your Father and has promised to take care of you on this earth. What dad would not provide for his children? God is with you and for you. He blesses you every day of your life. Yet, there's even more, immeasurably more: Heaven is our promised land, and it will be greater than we can imagine.

So reach out! Grab hold! Run with God and join in his work in this world! You get one shot, one opportunity, to live your life, so make the most of it. Do not settle for what this world has to offer; invest your life in Christ and his kingdom. Don't wait another minute! He is inviting you to truly experience the immeasurably more life. Now is the time. Live it!

Notes

1. Mark 4:11-12

2. 2 Kings 6:12

3. 2 Kings 6:15

4. 2 Kings 6:16

5. 2 Kings 6:17

6. 2 Kings 6:18

7. 2 Peter 3:8-9

8. Matthew 6:22-23

9. 2 Corinthians 5:7

10. Isaiah 14:12-14

11. 2 Corinthians 4:4

12. John 10:10

13. James 1:17

14. Mark 1:17

15. Matthew 22:2

16. Revelation 19

17. Matthew 22:3

18. Proverbs 22:6 (NKJV)

19. Romans 8:28

20. Genesis 12:1

21. Genesis 22:18 (NKJV)

22. Genesis 17:5

23. Luke 1:34

24. Luke 1:37 (HCSB)

25. Some of the names have been changed in this story.

26. Accounts of Jesus feeding the 5,000 can be found in all four gospels: John 6:1-15, Matthew 14:13-21, Mark 6:30-44, and Luke 9:10-17.

27. Matthew 7:7

28. This comes from Luke 22:42, when Jesus says, "Father, if you are willing, take this cup from me; yet not my will, but yours be done."

29. Taken from Jeremiah 29:11 - "For I know the plans I have for you," declares the LORD, "plans to prosper you and not to harm you, plans to give you hope and a future."

30. Matthew 7:7-11

31. Numbers 13:27

32. Deuteronomy 6:10-12

33. Isaiah 55:8

34. John 11:14-15

35. John 11:43

36. 1 Samuel 1:11-18

37. Galatians 5:22-23

38. Rick Jervis, "Mountains and planning lessened punch by Hurricane Patricia," USA Today, October 26, 2015, http://www.usatoday.com/story/news/world/2015/10/25/hurricane-patricia-mexico-impact/74592084/

39. 1 John 5:14

40. The names in this letter have been changed.

41. Gomer was married to Hosea in the Book of Hosea in the Bible. Hosea loved Gomer in spite of her love for other men. Many parallels have been made between the Israelites and God's pursuit of his people in spite of the fact that they chased after other gods.

42. James 5:17-18

43. John 14:12

44. 2 Corinthians 5:17 (NKJV)

45. Acts 7:60

46. Acts 9:3-5

47. Mark 8:36

48. Taken from Matthew 25:21

49. Genesis 2

50. Genesis 1

51. Matthew 22:37-40

52. Luke 10:33

53. James 1:2-4

54. 1 John 2:15-17

55. Exodus 20:3

56. Augustine: Confessions. Saint Augustine. Translated by Albert C. Outler. Accessed online at http://www.ccel.org/ccel/augustine/confessions.iv.html on February 4, 2016.

57. 1 Timothy 6:10

58. Matthew 6:24

59. Malachi 3:8-10

60. You can find a Financial Peace University class near you at www.daveramsey.com.

61. Psalm 46:10

62. Luke 1:37 (NKJV)

63. 2 Timothy 1:7 (NKJV)

64. McLean, Candis. "The Age of Anxiety." The Report Newsmagazine (Alberta Edition) 28.2 (2001): 42. Print.

65. Matthew 14:30

66. Matthew 14:31

67. Joshua 1:9

68. Romans 8:31

69. 1 John 4:18

70. Hebrews 13:5 (NKJV)

71. Matthew 11

72. John 20:25

73. Baird, J. (2014, September 25). Doubt as a Sign of Faith. The New York Times, Retrieved from http://www.nytimes.com/2014/09/26/opinion/julia-baird-doubt-as-a-sign-of-faith.html

74. Ibid.

75. Mark 9:21-22

76. Mark 9:23

77. Mark 9:24

78. 2 Corinthians 5:7

79. John 20:27

80. John 20:26

81. 1 John 1:9

82. Psalm 103:12

83. Hebrews 8:12

84. Acts 13:22

85. 1 Chronicles 29:11-12 (ESV)

86. Philippians 1:6

87. Job 1:21

88. Job 2:10

89. Proverbs 3:5-6

90. James 1:2-4

91. Malachi 2:16: "'The man who hates and divorces his wife,' says the Lord, the God of Israel, 'does violence to the one he should protect,' says the Lord Almighty. So be on your guard, and do not be unfaithful."

92. Mark 4:38

93. Mark 4:39-40

94. 2 Corinthians 9:15

95. John 16:33

96. 2 Corinthians 4:17

97. Romans 8:38-39

98. Isaiah 6:8

99. Matthew 17:20

100. Lisa Cannon Green. Finding Family in a Foreign Land. Baptist Press. December 11, 2015. http://www.bpnews.net/45989/finding-family-in-a-foreign-land

101. John 10:10

102. Matthew 6:27

103. James 1:5

104. Romans 8:29

105. Matthew 22:37-40

106. Psalm 86:11-13

107. Strength to Love, Martin Luther King, 1963

108. Deuteronomy 6:4-9

109. Hebrews 11

110. 1 Kings 11:3

111. Hebrews 12:1-3

112. 2 Timothy 4:7-8

113. Hebrews 13:5 (NKJV)

114. Matthew 28:19-20a

115. Matthew 28:20b

116. Daniel 3:16-18

117. Daniel 3:24-25

118. Daniel 3:26

119. Hebrews 13:5 (NKJV)

120. Isaiah 43:1-3

121. Matthew 1:23

122. Romans 8:31-38

123. Acts 1:10

124. Acts 1:11

125. 1 Thessalonians 5:16-18

126. 1 John 3:1

SPECIAL THANKS

As with any project, it takes a lot of people to make it happen. First, I want to thank our great God. Without Him, none of this happens. Thank you, Father, for inviting me on this journey with you. Thank you for redeeming my life through your Son, Jesus Christ, and giving me joy in the journey. I love You, and I love being a part of what You are doing! Next, I want to thank the incredible people of Rolling Hills Community Church. I love each and every one of you! This is our story together of God's amazing work in just a few short years. Thank you for praying and living our Christ each and every day. And, I still believe our best days are ahead. God's story is still being written and there are so many more people who need Jesus as we share His love, minister to those in our community as well as around the world and mature in our personal faith journey. In addition, I want to thank my beautiful, amazing wife without whom, none of this would be possible. When I was scared to death to step out in faith (even though I knew God was calling us) and to plant Rolling Hills, Lisa was always steadfast and had more faith than I did. She is an amazing wife, mom, creative and partner in ministry. I love you! Along with Lisa, I want to thank my three beautiful daughters, Grace, Mabry, and Kate. I love each of you, and it is such a blessing to be your earthly daddy. After this, the list is too long. From our amazing church staff team, who I love serving with each day and seeing miracles together, to our Justice & Mercy International Staff teams in the US, Moldova and the Amazon. What incredible, godly, and gifted men and women who are making a huge impact for the Kingdom. I love and appreciate you all! Then, there are specific people who have made this project happen like Julie Catron, Sara Ingmire, Nanette O'Grady, and Ana Monnaco. You all are the best! My God has put incredible people around me, and I am forever grateful. All glory to our great God!